Cambridge Elements

Elements in the Problems of God
edited by
Michael L. Peterson
Asbury Theological Seminary

GOD AND HUMAN GENETIC ENGINEERING

David Basinger
Roberts Wesleyan University

CAMBRIDGE
UNIVERSITY PRESS

CAMBRIDGE
UNIVERSITY PRESS

Shaftesbury Road, Cambridge CB2 8EA, United Kingdom

One Liberty Plaza, 20th Floor, New York, NY 10006, USA

477 Williamstown Road, Port Melbourne, VIC 3207, Australia

314–321, 3rd Floor, Plot 3, Splendor Forum, Jasola District Centre,
New Delhi – 110025, India

103 Penang Road, #05–06/07, Visioncrest Commercial, Singapore 238467

Cambridge University Press is part of Cambridge University Press & Assessment,
a department of the University of Cambridge.

We share the University's mission to contribute to society through the pursuit of
education, learning and research at the highest international levels of excellence.

www.cambridge.org
Information on this title: www.cambridge.org/9781009467889

DOI: 10.1017/9781009269360

First published 2023

A catalogue record for this publication is available from the British Library

ISBN 978-1-009-46788-9 Hardback
ISBN 978-1-009-26934-6 Paperback
ISSN 2754-8724 (online)
ISSN 2754-8716 (print)

God and Human Genetic Engineering

Elements in the Problems of God

DOI: 10.1017/9781009269360
First published online: November 2023

David Basinger
Roberts Wesleyan University

Author for correspondence: David Basinger, basingerd@roberts.edu

Abstract: Science and Religion have often intersected on issues. However, no set of current scientific advances is more promising and problematic for religious (or nonreligious) individuals than those that fall under the heading of Human Genetic Engineering, as these advances have the potential not only to cure human disease, remove undesirable human traits, and enhance desirable human traits but also to pass on these modifications to future generations. This Element is an introductory overview of these advances, the ethical issues they raise, and the lines of reasoning, including religious lines of reasoning, used to support or challenge these advances. The author's goal is to suggest a way of assessing these advances that will give us, whether religious or not, a solid basis for deciding these issues for ourselves and engaging in respectful, constructive dialog with others.

This Element also has a video abstract: www.Cambridge.org/Basigner

Keywords: genetic engineering, god and science, changing humans, CRISPR, modifying DNA

ISBNs: 9781009467889 (HB), 9781009269346 (PB), 9781009269360 (OC)
ISSNs: 2754-8724 (online), 2754-8716 (print)

Contents

1 Science and Religion: Is There a Conflict?

The scientific method is "the process of objectively establishing facts through testing and experimentation. The basic process involves making an observation, forming a hypothesis, making a prediction, conducting an experiment and finally analyzing the results" (Wright & Lavery, n.d.).

That this method has transformed and continues to transform the way we understand our world and act accordingly is beyond doubt. It is true that those who identify themselves as religious tend to trust science less than those who don't when asked to rate their level of trust, although this level of trust differs around the world. "The perceived disparity between faith and science was highest in parts of Asia, with 64 percent of Christians in South Korea and 58 percent of Christians in Singapore reporting some conflict. It was lowest in Sweden, where just 15 percent of Christians saw conflict" (Shellnutt, 2020).

However, most religious individuals by their actions demonstrate significant trust in a scientific understanding of everything from how the body works and what we should do to regain/retain health, the types of cars we should drive and how they should be driven, how we should grow the food we eat and how that food should be consumed, and why we behave the way we do and how we should interact with each other accordingly.

In short, conflicts between science and religion are seldom based on the belief that the scientific method as a means of understanding our world is inherently flawed or even on the belief that this method doesn't give us very helpful information about our world and how we should act within it the majority of the time. Actual conflicts arise when some who identify as religious believe there is another source of truth about our world, namely some form of divine/supernatural revelation. More specifically, conflicts arise for individuals when the truth about some aspect of our world is believed to have been revealed to them through sacred texts, the ability to discern truth through direct communication with the divine, and/or truth from the divine transmitted through trusted spiritual leaders is inconsistent with what they believe science is telling them about this aspect of our world.

The classic historical example is the conflict between Galileo's scientific belief that the earth revolves around the sun and the church's revelatory belief that the earth was the center of the universe. Another well-known example that still exists for some religious individuals is the conflict between the scientific belief that the universe began as just a single point about 13.7 billion years ago and has been expanding ever since and the revelatory belief that the universe was created *ex nihilo* (out of nothing) by God around 10,000 years ago.

Some conflicts based on competing sources of truth clearly remain today. For example, the scientific belief that there are fully natural explanations for all we experience conflicts with the revelatory belief that God at times intervenes in the natural order to bring about some state of affairs that would not have occurred as it did without some form of "supernatural" action.

However, we do not find this type of conflict related to genetic engineering – the process by which DNA in our cells can be modified to bring about changes in our bodies. That is, there are not, to my knowledge, any competing religious truth claims concerning the role that cells play in organisms, the roles that genes and DNA play in our cells, our ability to modify genes and thus cells in ways that impact the health and behavior of organisms, the increasingly sophisticated tools being developed to modify genes, or the increasing impact such modification can have on the future of humanity. There are, of course, differences of opinion on all of this within the scientific community. However, these disagreements aren't based on religious versus scientific sources of truth. They are based on differing views on the science (the empirical data) and are as likely to arise among individuals (e.g., scientists) who happen to be religious and those who aren't. We seldom, though, find religious individuals challenging the claims of science in this arena on revelatory grounds.

However, isn't there a conflict between science and religion at an ethical (ought) level? Don't science and religion conflict on the question of the extent, if any, to which it is ethically justifiable to engage in genetic engineering? As we will soon discuss in great detail, this is a very complex question. While it is, of course, true that those individuals who are religious often have at least in part a different basis (a revelatory basis) for the ethical principles that guide their thoughts and actions related to what is right or wrong than those individuals who are not religious, the actual ethical principles that guide the thinking of nonreligious individuals on ethical issues related to genetic engineering issues are often exactly the same ethical principles that guide the thinking of religious individuals on these issues. Or, to state this important point differently, in relation to the topic at hand, it isn't even the case that the vast majority (or even in some cases the majority) who are nonreligious (including most scientists who are nonreligious) affirm significantly different ethical principles from the vast majority of those who are religious (including most scientists who are religious) on these issues.

This doesn't mean that religion is irrelevant to an analysis of genetic engineering. It simply means, as we will see, that the relevance is different from and much more nuanced than our normal understanding of conflicts between science and religion.

2 Genetic Engineering and Religious Belief: How Ought We View Their Relationship?

There are various related, but distinct, ways of describing the relationship between genetic engineering and religion. Sometimes this relationship is approached as a comparative study of the percent of those adhering to various religions (or to no religion at all) who hold a certain position on genetic engineering in general or some specific aspect of genetic engineering.

For example, from one poll we learn that "57% of Protestants (62% of Evangelicals) oppose [genetic engineering technology] based on their religious or ethical views while 37% are in favor; Catholics followed closely behind with 52% opposed and 42% in favor. Among Muslims, 46% are opposed, with 32% in favor. Jews had the most favorable view of the technology, with 55% in favor and 35% opposed" (AgBiotechNet, 2001).

Another, more narrowly focused study of this type compared the views of Christians in twenty countries with their nonreligious neighbors on gene-editing technology. It was found, overall, that "believers lag behind non-religious neighbors in support for the technology." More specifically, the study showed that "Christians in the US are half as likely as the religiously unaffiliated to believe scientific research on gene editing is an appropriate use of technology (21% vs. 47%), the widest gap among the countries surveyed." In Canada, the UK, the Netherlands, Sweden, Italy, and Spain, believers "also lagged behind the unaffiliated, though both demographics disapproved of gene-editing research." In France, "where approval levels were lowest, Christians and the unaffiliated felt about the same (16% vs. 15% said it was appropriate)." Finally, "few people, regardless of faith, considered it appropriate to alter genetic makeup to make a baby more intelligent; overall, 82 percent disapproved" (Shellnutt, 2020).

While interesting, this type of demographic information, itself, tells us very little about the relationship between religious belief and genetic engineering. The fact that someone who is affiliated with a religion holds a certain view on an issue doesn't mean that the perspective held by the person is based on a religious belief – a belief grounded in the teachings or set of doctrines of the religion affirmed by this person. Some religious individuals hold their positions because they trust what they are told is true by respected religious authorities while others just intuit or sense what is right. In other words, we must make the important distinction between individuals who are religious and take a stance for and against an issue that doesn't have any obvious, direct basis in the person's religious beliefs/commitments and individuals who are religious and take a stance for or against an issue that does have its basis in a religious intuition/belief/commitment the person holds. Furthermore, even if we assume that the person's perspective on an issue is grounded in what the person understands to be beliefs (tenets) of the religion in question, such polling doesn't identify for us what these beliefs are.

It is more helpful in this regard if surveys or studies give us insight into the specific religious beliefs that impact a religious person's views on genetic engineering – for instance, the belief that it is wrong to "play God" and that those involved in human genetic engineering are playing God.

Some studies address part of this concern. For instance, a Pew Research Center poll measured the percent "of U.S. adults who say gene editing to give babies a much reduced risk of serious diseases and conditions" is either "no different than other ways we try to better ourselves" or "crosses a line, is meddling with nature." An interesting finding was that the response of those who were religious differed significantly in relation to their standing on a religious commitment index – for example, on the frequency of prayer, the frequency of attendance at religious meetings, and how important religion is self-reported to be to them. While only 33 percent of those who were high on the index believed that the genetic editing of babies to reduce disease is no different than other ways we try to better ourselves, 49 percent of those who were medium on the index and 70 percent of those who were low on the index thought this to be the case (Pew Research Center, 2016a).

It is reasonable to assume that this correlation between index status and response can be attributed in part to the fact that those who are high on the religious commitment index ground their views more firmly in the teachings (beliefs) of their religion than do those who are medium or low on the index. We still, however, don't learn from such studies which religious beliefs are responsible for this impact.

This limitation is in one sense addressed by those studies attempting to determine how the recognized (or sanctioned) beliefs of a religion relate to genetic engineering in general or specific aspects of this technology. In fact, some studies not only identify the key relevant beliefs of religions but do so in a comparative manner.

For example, one study shows that "a majority in all religious groups believes that humans should use their knowledge to improve the life of other humans." In response to the question of whether God has empowered humans to use science to improve life or whether humans are "playing God," what surfaced was that "a majority of all those polled felt [humans have] been empowered by God to improve life. Jews and Muslims agreed the most strongly with the statement on empowerment (62% and 61% agreed, respectively), followed by Catholics (55%) and Protestants (54%)" (AgBiotechNet, 2001).

Additionally, most polled, regardless of religion, felt that it is important to "improve the world or strike a balance between improving and preserving it. Jewish adults feel most strongly that humans have an obligation to improve the world (60%). Protestants are more likely than other religious groups to say that humans should strike a balance (43%), with nearly half of born-again Christians (48%) saying humans should strike a balance" (Pew Trust, 2001).

More recently, a study compared and contrasted the perspectives of Christianity, Judaism, Hinduism, Buddhism, and Islam on a variety of bio-ethical issues, including gene editing. Among the key findings was that while Judaism encourages caution in applying biotechnology, there appears to be "nothing prohibiting one from engaging in research and development ... so long as policy makers and regulators take care to assure that the technology is put to beneficial use with appropriate safeguards." Muslim and Hindu perspectives are similar: "there are no particular principles that could be seen as a basis for prohibiting biotech development." More specifically, Buddhism, Judaism, Islam, and Hinduism consider an embryo a human life but are generally accepting of human embryonic stem cell research. Overall, the Christian perspective on biotechnology is more negative, especially among those Christians who believe life begins at conception and, thus, oppose any technology (such as embryonic research or editing) that normally results in the destruction of human embryos (Warmflash, 2019).

I still have a concern. Everyone agrees, including those conducting the polling in question, that there exists a variety of perspectives within any given religion. There is often an assumption, though, that there is in every religion a substantial set of core beliefs (doctrines) that are shared by most adherents to any given religion and that we can, therefore, look to these core theological and ethical beliefs when determining the stance of a religion on issues related to genetic engineering.

This seems to me a dubious assumption. First, as we'll discuss in greater detail in Section 7.2.2, even if we assume there to be a set of core beliefs affirmed by most adherents in a religion, there is no guarantee that these adherents will agree on how these core beliefs should be applied now (or in the future) to genetic engineering.

The more significant problem here, as I see it, is the questionable assumption that there is, even at the most fundamental, general level, one set of sanctioned core beliefs for a religion. As I have stated elsewhere,

> while there is obviously widespread diversity of thought among these mono-theistic religions (theistic systems) on such fundamental issues as God's nature and character, the relationship between divine control and human

freedom, the extent to which God unilaterally intervenes in our world, and how God would have us live, it is being increasingly recognized that widespread diversity of thought on all these issues also exists just as clearly, and in exactly the same sense, *within* religions. (Basinger, 2020a)

In fact, the perspective of a variant of a given religion on an issue is often more closely aligned with the perspective of variants of differing religions than with the perspective of other variants of the given religion in question. The stance of conservative Christians, for instance, is often more similar to the stance of conservative Muslims or conservative Jews than the stance of more liberal Christians. And this holds for issues related to genetic engineering – for example, on why disease exists and the acceptable methods for addressing it.

How then ought we to proceed? The best approach, I believe, is to consider the religious beliefs that actually serve as the basis for religious responses to genetic engineering without attempting to tie such beliefs to any specific religion or even a variant of a religion. Since most, if not all, of the religious beliefs we will consider are both affirmed and denied by proponents of variants within most religions, not tying any given belief to any given religion will allow us to assess such beliefs without making any determination about the "official" stance of any actual religion or its variant on the issues in question.

Or stated differently, while I will at times note what are seen by some as the basic tenets (sanctioned beliefs) of various religions and the views held by individuals who self-report as being affiliated with these religions or their variants, our main goal is to explore the religious beliefs (beliefs that have a religious basis) and related lines of reasoning on genetic engineering, regardless of the religion variants in which these beliefs are found or the extent to which individuals who self-report as religious or affiliated with a variant of a religion actually affirm these religious beliefs and related arguments. I will in conclusion, though, also share what I see as the most constructive approach to the current, often contentious religious dialog around these issues.

3 Genetic Engineering: An Overview

Genetic engineering focuses on genes, but what exactly are genes and what role do they play in the life of an organism? All organisms are comprised of a variety of cells that work together to help the organism function. In every cell is a molecule called DNA, which is specific to that organism (unless the organism has an identical twin). Genes are short sections of DNA in a cell that control the function that cell plays in the life of the organism. Humans, for example, have hundreds of different kinds of cells, each of which carries out the instructions from its genes to keep our various bodily systems functioning. In this role, genes carry DNA instructions that determine, among other things, our eye and hair color and are contributing factors to such things as our weight, blood pressure, and cholesterol levels (Genes & Health, n.d.).

Genetic engineering is an attempt to alter the DNA within a gene to change the makeup of an organism – a plant, animal, or human. The most common and least controversial form of genetic engineering is that which is intended to "fix" a problem within an organism. This form of genetic engineering, often referred to as gene therapy, has as its goal to return a faulty gene (DNA) in a cell to its "normal" state.[1] This can be accomplished in three ways.

Gene inhibition therapy seeks to "eliminate the activity of a gene that encourages the growth of disease-related cells" (Yg Topics, 2021). Such therapy is used to treat cancer or inherited disorders. It's also used to treat those cancers resulting from the over-activation of certain genes. "By eliminating the activity of that [gene] through gene inhibition therapy, it is possible to prevent further cell growth and stop the cancer in its tracks" (Yg Topics, 2021). Gene augmentation therapy seeks to add a "healthy copy of a gene to a cell where a faulty gene exists, so the healthy copy can override the negative effects caused by the faulty gene" (Gragnolati, 2022). This type of therapy is used to treat functional disorders such as cystic fibrosis. Finally, gene-killing therapy attempts to "insert DNA instructions into an unhealthy cell that causes the cell to die" (Yg Topics, 2021). This type of therapy is used to treat certain cancers.

There is, though, a different form of genetic engineering that is not intended to fix a problem with the genes in a cell but rather to modify the genes (DNA) in a cell – that is, to add, change, or remove certain DNA sequences in a cell – in order to increase the likelihood that the organism will exhibit some desired (enhanced) trait. This form of genetic manipulation is common at the plant level and becoming more common at the animal level as an alleged means to increase the quality and quantity of our food supply without increasing cost or harming the environment. As we will see, this form of enhancement engineering, while not yet widespread at the human level, is increasingly becoming the subject of intense scientific and ethical debate (Missouri School of Medicine, n.d.).

Before discussing the application of the various forms of genetic engineering in more detail, I want to introduce two relevant distinctions and also CRISPR: the recent gene-editing technique that has greatly increased our ability to edit genes in ways that hold great promise for all but raise (or heighten) significant ethical concerns for many.

---

[1] While the focus of this Element will be on DNA editing, it's important to note in passing that RNA is another molecule in cells that converts the genetic information contained within DNA to a format used to build proteins. RNA editing is also gaining in popularity and importance (Reardon, 2020).

One key distinction is between nonreproductive cells (somatic cells) and reproductive cells (germline cells). The modification of somatic cells will (hopefully) last for the life span of the organism but won't be passed on to offspring of the organism (the changes are not inheritable) while the successful modification of germline cells will be passed on to the offspring of the organism (the changes are inheritable.) Not surprisingly, it is germline genetic engineering that has generated the greatest ethical concerns (Evans, 2021).

The other key distinction focuses on the source of the DNA used in cell modification. Most genetically modified organisms (GMOs) with which we are all familiar at the plant level are genetically modified by injecting DNA from *another* organism. However, the type of genetic engineering increasingly common today does not introduce DNA from another organism. The organism's own DNA is edited.

This brings us to CRISPR, the exciting, relatively new technique that has revolutionized the way in which we edit (modify) an organism's own genes.

An acronym for "clustered regularly interspaced short palindromic repeats," CRISPR was adapted from a naturally occurring genome editing system and unveiled in 2012. Other gene-editing techniques have been in use for decades. However, CRISPR has made such editing faster, cheaper, and more accurate than other modern genome editing techniques. This technique can be used to introduce DNA from another organism. It's best known, though, for its ability to allow us to locate a specific piece of DNA inside a cell and then alter the DNA sequence or turn genes on or off without altering the sequence. And since the changes are made to the DNA within the cells of an organism, as opposed to changes made by introducing DNA from another organism into the cell, the changes are more easily reproduced as the edited cells divide (NewScientist, 2022).

The potential impact of this technique on our future as humans cannot be overemphasized. Larry Locke states that "unless you were around to witness the development of immunology by Louis Pasteur in the 1870s, it is hard to imagine a biotechnology that has generated more acclamation than CRISPR" (Locke, 2020). Carolyn Brokowski and Mazhar Adli note that CRISPR technology is "the most versatile genomic engineering tool created in the history of molecular biology to date" (Brokowski & Adli, 2019). And in the words of Jennifer Doudna, who along with Emmanuel Charpentier "discovered" CRISPR, "The power to control our species' genetic future is awesome and terrifying. Deciding how to handle it may be the biggest challenge we have ever faced" (Doudna & Sternberg, 2017, p. 240).

3.1 Genetic Engineering: Plants

This Element is primarily focused on the genetic engineering *of* humans. However, I'm going to briefly extend this discussion to the genetic engineering of plants and animals because of the impact such engineering does and increasingly will have *on* humans.

When we think of genetically modified plants (food), we normally think of GMOs. As we've seen, GMOs are organisms that have had their DNA genetically altered primarily by adding or inserting genes from other organisms. Currently most commercially available genetically modified food stuffs are GMOs. However, the use of CRISPR, which doesn't insert DNA from other plants but rather edits the DNA within a plant, is gaining popularity. For example, using CRISPR to modify a gene in an apple, rather than the normal GMO technique that introduces foreign DNA, makes slices less likely to turn brown (Synthego, n.d.).

While various plants can and have been genetically modified, the major impact has been on crop plants. The three major crop plants genetically modified are corn, soybeans, and cotton, although such staples as potatoes, canola, alfalfa, apples, and sugar beets are also modified. The impact is pervasive in scope. In most cases, the majority of a crop has been altered. In some cases, over 90 percent of what is planted today is genetically modified (US Department of Agriculture, 2022).

The debate continues, though, over whether we ought to use (or continue to use) genetically modified crops in this way, with the "experts" on each side offering what they see as strong arguments (Conserve Future Energy, n.d.). Those favoring the continued and even expanded use of genetic engineering argue that genetically modified crops:

- Last longer and thus limit waste as there is more time for usable distribution.
- Are more resistant to pests, weeds, and disease, and thus have greater yields, which in turn means it is possible to grow more food on existing crop land.
- Need fewer pesticides and other chemicals and are thus better for the environment.
- Need less water and so can be grown in regions with less rainfall or irrigation.
- Are at least as nutritious, if not more so, than non-GMO foods.
- Are no more dangerous to health than non-GMO foods.

Those favoring diminished reliance on genetic modification argue that genetically modified crops:

- Are not necessarily safe. For instance, we can't yet be certain that GMOs won't increase allergic reactions or even cause (trigger) some forms of cancer.
- Have built-in pesticides (in GMOs) that may well produce "super bugs" that will be pesticide-resistant.

- Can lead to monopolies (and thus higher prices) since only a few companies hold most of the patents. This also makes it difficult to engage in independent studies.
- Produce certain weeds that are resistant to herbicides and thus farmers can still lose crops.
- Create legal difficulties for farmers with GMO crops in fields near fields on which GMO crops are not grown since the GMO seeds can spread to these fields and GMO farmers have been held liable for compensation.

As we see, the arguments on both sides focus primarily on a cost-benefit analysis. Those supporting the increasing use of genetic engineering on plants (especially crops) argue that the pervasive use of this technology is clearly on balance good for humans and the environment, while those who argue for a diminished role for such genetic manipulation maintain just the opposite.

Most religious discussions of genetic engineering in the plant realm are similar in nature. Assuming as a normative religious principle that we ought to care for our environment and attempt to better the lives of the individuals inhabiting this environment, discussions focus primarily on the relative benefits and risks involved.

There is, though, one additional religious component in these discussions: the tension between the religious principle that we ought not to tamper too significantly with the natural processes in God's creation and the religious principle that "we have been empowered by God to understand nature and use science and technology to improve the human condition," including the natural environment in which we live (AgBiotechNet, 2001). While we will discuss this tension in greater detail later, I want to note now that many religious individuals struggle to find the right balance between these two fundamental religious principles in this and related contexts.

3.2 Genetic Engineering: Animals

Humans have been modifying animals for thousands of years to produce desired traits, mainly by selective breeding and cross-breeding. For example, dogs have been selectively bred for such traits as speed, reflexes, stamina, strong senses, trainability, size, strength, low gravity, and agreeableness. Cattle have been selectively bred for climate tolerance, increased size and muscle mass, increased milk production and udder size, and increased fat and protein content. Modifying animals in this manner, however, takes time and is inexact. By contrast, in the past few decades, we have been able to genetically engineer animals by directly modifying their DNA in a more exact and timely fashion. Animals that have been safely genetically engineered in research settings include cattle, pigs, chickens, goats, sheep, dogs, cats, fish, rats, and mice (Innovation, n.d.).

Current genetic engineering of animals as it relates to humans falls into at least four basic categories: for use in research, as a source of food, as a source of organs/tissues for humans needing transplants, and as a method for preventing human disease.

We use genetically engineered animals in research labs to learn more about the genes of the animals in question or for biomedical testing. Most often used for lab testing are mice and rats, but such animals as rabbits, sheep, and goats are also used in this manner. A key focus of concern in this area is the treatment of the animals being modified, with some arguing that what the animals must endure is unjustified and others arguing that we should, at the very least, encourage the "refinement of tests so animal distress or pain is minimal," and that there be a "reduction of the number of animals used in a study and the replacement, whenever possible, of animal experiments with non-animal experiments" (American Human, 2021).

This concern appears to be shared by both religious and nonreligious individuals, although many religious individuals will again face the tension between their beliefs that we ought not engage in excessive tampering with our natural environment while we ought to use our knowledge of our natural environment for good.

Turning now to the use of genetic research on animals in food production, one noteworthy goal is to reduce the negative impact of the animals we use for food on the natural environment. An example of such modification is the Enviro-Pig™. Through genetic engineering, this pig emits 30 to 60 percent less phosphorus (which can have a negative impact on ecosystems) than traditional pigs fed the same conventional diet (Innovation, n.d.).

The main goal, though, is to modify animals in ways that will allow us to increase the supply of food without an increase (or with a decrease) in the necessary resources. Examples abound. Cows are being developed to produce more milk. Scientists from South China are developing pigs that grow faster with less negative impact on the environment (Cohen, 2019). The genetic modification of poultry has the potential to increase the rate of maturity and, thus, shorten the time between birth and market (increase the availability of food for consumption) while diminishing the necessary resources (mainly food and water).

While most genetic modification of this sort is still at the research stage and may stay there for some time, two genetically modified animals have been approved for human consumption. In 2019, genetically modified salmon – which are injected with DNA from other fish species that allows them to grow to full size faster – were approved for human consumption (Living Oceans, n.d.).

Also, in spring 2022, the FDA "announced that beef from two gene-edited cattle and their offspring is safe to eat and said gene-edited beef could be on the market in as little as two years." These cattle were designed using CRISPR "to grow shorter hair to better tolerate heat, which makes them more efficient for meat producers in hotter climates." It is expected that such announcements "will encourage more companies to bring forward gene-edited farm animals for marketplace approval in the near future" (Torrella, 2022).

As with plants, the genetic modification of animals for consumption falls into two categories: those cases in which the DNA from one animal is inserted into another animal and those cases in which the DNA within an animal is altered. Modified salmon are an example of the external insertion of DNA, while modified cattle are an example of internal cell DNA modification. We should expect more animals for human consumption based on internal cell modification techniques like CRISPR since editing an animal's genes rather than moving a gene from one animal into another is faster and more precise.

The debate continues, however, over whether we ought to use (or continue to use) genetically modified animals as a food source. While few question the obvious benefit of increasing food production without the need for additional resources, there is concern over the impact this will have on the genetically modified animals themselves. As some see it, the increasing use of gene editing to push chickens, pigs, fish, and cows to grow bigger and faster will place factory farming on overdrive, almost certainly to the detriment of animal welfare. There is the fear that even if some farms focus initially on easing animal suffering, this will "open up the floodgates for a lot of gene interventions that have very negative impacts on animal welfare" (Torrella, 2022).

Others maintain that such modification can alleviate some animal suffering. The creation of hornless calves, they point out, has eliminated the need for the painful yet common farm procedure known as dehorning. It's also likely that animals can be bred to be disease-resistant, which could lead agribusiness to breed fewer animals overall. In fact, advancements in genetic engineering may well enable diseases to be detected and cured before birth, thus paving the way for all animals to be born stronger and healthier (StopGM, 2019).

Another example of modification intended in part to alleviate animal suffering is the genetic engineering of chicks that is being done to help limit or eliminate the practice of killing millions of male chicks since they can't lay eggs and have been bred to be too small to be worth the effort of raising for meat. Researchers in Australia are using CRISPR to insert a gene from a sea anemone into a chicken egg that expresses a particular protein; if it's a male, the inside of the egg will glow red when a laser is shined on it, enabling egg producers to destroy the eggs before the chicks are hatched (Torrella, 2022). A team in the UK is working to stop the development of male embryos (Corbyn, 2021).

Even if we grant that animal suffering can be alleviated, some will still argue that we should reduce or suspend the genetic modification of animals for human consumption until more is known. Scientists know much about the animal body and how it works, but they don't yet understand everything. Specifically, the risk factors related to modifying an animal at the cellular level are widely unknown, and there could be many risks to doing this that we are just unaware of at the moment. By making a seemingly positive change, scientists could end up with unintended negative results. We need more focused research on this issue, it is argued, before the wide-scale research continues (StopGM, 2019).

When considering the value of genetically engineered animals to address the growing shortage of available organs for transplant in humans, the focus remains primarily on the domestic pig, which we have known for decades to be an optimum donor for such transplants because "their relevant organs are a similar size to humans ... and because pigs are relatively easy to breed and raise in captivity" (Hunter, 2022). The technical problem is clear: because humans and pigs are different species, pig-to-human transplant "involves high immune incompatibility and a complex rejection process." However, "the rapid development of genetic engineering techniques enables genome modifications in pigs that reduce the cross-species immune barrier" (Hryhorowicz et al., 2017). One such technique involves the use of genetically altered pig cells to produce embryos that when birthed and raised in a bio-sealed environment have. organs that are less likely to be rejected when implanted in humans.

Some progress along these lines continues. In January 2020, a severely ill man became the first to receive a pig heart during an operation. The man survived the surgery but died two months later, perhaps because of a pathogen in the pig heart. In late 2021, surgeons transferred kidneys from pigs into "two legally dead people who had no discernible brain function. The kidneys functioned normally over the 54 hours of the test and seemed to produce urine" (Kozlov, 2022). Applications for formal clinical trials have been submitted to the FDA.

The benefit for humans is obvious: a sufficient supply of organs and tissues to meet the current need. Should we not, though, be concerned with the lives of the modified pigs (or other animals genetically modified for this use)? As some animal rights advocates see it, "animals have a right to live their lives, without being genetically manipulated with all the pain and trauma this entails, only to be killed and their organs harvested" (Hunter, 2022). A common response is that unless using pigs (or other animals) for food is not justifiable, then it's difficult to see why this use of pigs (or other animals) is problematic. A middle ground is that we only use gene-edited pigs for organs if we can "ensure they do not suffer unnecessary harm." The fact that we use pigs to produce meat is "no reason to ignore animal welfare" in this area (Hunter, 2022).

There is in this context also a specifically religious concern that needs to be addressed. Pigs are, as noted, presently the primary source of animal organs/ tissue. However, both Muslims and Jews have strict rules on the use of certain animals, which includes a ban on the raising or eating of pigs. While that ban holds, Jews and Muslims both allow the use of porcine products in medicines and vaccines. Furthermore, both allow the use of pig valves in heart surgery. So there appears to be no special problem with the use of pig organs for transplant. The general principle in both religions (and their variants) seems to be that the use of interspecies transplant is acceptable if necessary to cure human illnesses if no other means is available (Rosner, 1999).

We genetically modify pigs for organ transplant to address significant health concerns humans are already facing: diseased kidneys, faulty heart values, and so on. There is, though, another area of germline genetic research that has as its goal the prevention of health concerns (disease) in humans, namely, the gene-editing of mosquitoes (which as insects are animals).

Over one million individuals die each year from mosquito-borne diseases, with malaria alone causing over 400,000 deaths per year (mostly among children). Moreover, "mosquitoes are increasingly becoming resistant to pesticides, and the parasite that causes malaria is also becoming increasingly resistant to the antimalarial drugs" (Dunning, 2021). Very promising gene-editing work is being done on mosquitoes to spread infertility that would eliminate the species or produce a malaria-blocking gene (Dunning, 2021).

No one (religious or not) denies that saving of lives of over a million individuals would be a great good. Some maintain, however, that while "the eradication of mosquitoes might please humans in the short term, [it] would eventually damage many ecosystems due to a cascade of negative consequences as more and more species were affected" (Arcata, 2021). It has been argued, for example, that "in places with many flying biting insects, cattle, horses and other large grazers spend parts of the day resting in dusty, vegetation-free areas that are exposed to the wind, as a means of gaining respite from [mosquitoes]" so eradicating mosquitoes "could remove a behavioural constraint on these herbivores that would enable them to graze for longer in areas that are currently only tolerable for short periods of time due to the fly density" (Wallace, 2021). For such individuals, regional eradication is more appealing.

A more general cautionary comment is that since we don't yet know the potentially negative impact of what would replace the mosquito, we need to move slowly at this point.

Also, for those religious individuals who believe God is directly responsible for the creation of every animal for a specific purpose, to purposely eradicate a species might be an inappropriate tampering with God's creation and foolish since there clearly is a divine purpose for mosquitoes, whether or not we as humans will ever discover exactly what that is (Eikelboom, 2011).

Finally, there are some general concerns related to the genetic engineering of animals that hold regardless of the focus or purpose of such research. Those who believe that animals have moral standing (rights) apart from their value to humans see all forms of genetic research on animals as very problematic since such engineering reduces animals to mere machines to be fine-tuned for our benefit alone. Others are opposed to such research in general as they see this as opening the door for significant genetic abuse and misuse in the future.

4 Genetic Engineering: Humans

Up to this point, we have limited our discussion of genetic engineering to its most literal sense: the altering of the DNA within a gene to change the makeup of an organism. In our discussion of human genetic engineering, however, we're going to use a broader understanding that includes the duplication of human genes (cloning) and the increasing use of "genetic information" (genetic counseling, testing, and screening) to make decisions about human life.

I'm doing so because I believe most individuals, including most religious individuals, usually have this extended understanding in mind when thinking about genetic engineering. More importantly, both cloning and the use of genetic information are related to the impact of genetics on human life, which is in its most basic sense what this Element is about.

I'm going to divide human genetic engineering in this extended sense into two categories: those types of engineering related to preconception and prenatal (reproductive) processes and those types related to genetically interventive processes after birth. Genetic engineering after birth is the genetic editing of nonreproductive (somatic) cells and can be used either to prevent or to stop disease or to restore diseased cells to normalcy or to enhance human traits. We'll start by considering the preventative/restorative uses of gene editing (gene therapy) as these are more prevalent and less controversial.

4.1 Somatic Human Gene Editing: Preventative/Restorative

Scientists have been working for decades on ways to modify genes or replace faulty genes with healthy ones to treat, cure, or prevent a disease or medical condition. Work started in the 1980s, with the first success in 1990 when a four-year old girl born with a severe combined immunodeficiency (SCID) had a healthy gene inserted into her blood cells that resolved the problem and has allowed her to live a normal life. Then in the 1990s, a series of setbacks slowed work in this area.

Since the mid-2000s, gene therapy has experienced a renaissance as we have continued at a rapid rate to gain a more detailed, comprehensive understanding of cell function and create better gene-editing tools such as CRISPR (Fliesler, 2020).

As already noted, in the most general sense, the gene therapies of today can or will soon be able to replace, turn off, or modify the genes in our cells. More specifically, using gene therapy, we can or will hopefully soon be able to do the following (Mayo Clinic, n.d.):

- Introduce a new or modified gene into the cell to help treat a disease. Sometimes the whole or part of a gene is defective or missing from birth. Or cells can be diseased because genes have mutated or simply stop working correctly or working at all. Replacing the defective genes with healthy copies can help cells function normally.
- Inactivate (turn off) a faulty gene that is causing (supporting) disease.
- Activate (turn on) healthy genes that will help prevent disease.
- Make diseased cells more evident to the immune system. In some cases, immune systems don't attack diseased cells because they aren't recognized as threats. Gene therapy can be used to train the immune system to recognize the cells that need to be attacked.

Genetic material and gene-editing tools can't simply (or successfully) be inserted directly into a cell. Instead, we use genetically engineered carriers called "vectors" to carry and deliver what's needed. The most common vectors at present are certain viruses, which are modified to deliver the material or tools without directly or inadvertently harming the cell.

When we want to deliver what's needed into cells in the body, we normally use an injection or IV to introduce the materials or tools "into a specific tissue in the body, where [they are] taken up by individual cells" (MedlinePlus, n.d.).

We do, though, at times, also introduce material and tools into cells outside the body by exposing them to the vector in a laboratory setting. The cells to be exposed can come from the patient (autologous cells) or a donor (allogeneic cells). The cells containing the vector are then returned to the patient. Or, to be more specific, in gene therapy that is used to modify cells outside of the body, blood, bone marrow, or another tissue can be taken from a patient or a donor, and specific types of cells can be separated out in the lab. The vector containing the desired gene is introduced into these cells. The cells are left to multiply in the laboratory and then injected into the patient, where they continue to multiply and eventually produce the desired effect (UFDA, 2022).

While viral vectors are the most commonly used, they aren't the only vector options. Nonviral vectors used to carry altered genes into your body's cells include (1) chemical vectors that are inorganic particles, lipid-based, polymer-based, and peptide-based and (2) physical vectors, such as electroporation, sonoporation, photoporation, and magnetofection (Ramamoorth & Narvekar, 2015).

The types of diseases or abnormal conditions on which somatic gene therapy is focused today include sickle cell disease, severe hemophilia A, hemophilia B, different cancers such as acute lymphoblastic leukemia, certain forms of blindness, ophthalmic and neurologic problems, obesity, high blood pressure, and high cholesterol. There are at present over 1,000 ongoing gene therapy clinical trials (Kelmer & Lohr, 2022). Moreover, while treatments were only available in clinical trials until 2017 (Kelmer & Lohr, 2022), today more than twenty gene therapy products have been approved for availability on the open market for such conditions as spinal muscular atrophy, inherited retinal dystrophy, a number of forms of leukemia, and lymphoma. Some believe that "in the next 5–8 years … up to 70 cell and gene products could be approved" (Melillo, 2022).

The benefits of the types of somatic preventative or restorative gene therapy we have been considering are obvious. Such therapy has the real potential to "cure" diseases and conditions that we simply haven't been able to address adequately with current approaches, including medications. Also, while there are some conditions that can be managed with repeated doses of medication, gene therapy, as it normally makes permanent changes in cells, has the potential to be a onetime process that will do away with a person's symptoms for life.

4.1.1 Preventative/Restorative Somatic Editing: Concerns

There are, however, concerns with preventative and restorative somatic gene therapy, with many centering on the risks associated with such procedures. Some fear that vector viruses will trigger a dangerous immune response. For instance, the body's immune system may see the newly introduced viruses as intruders and attack them, which in turn can cause inflammation and, in severe cases, organ failure. While this potential problem has been greatly minimized, it remains a real possibility. There is also the possibility that the virus carriers will cause an infection or, once introduced into the body, recover their original ability to cause disease.

Others are worried that the wrong cells might be targeted. Because viruses can affect more than one type of cells, it's possible that the altered viruses may infect additional cells – not just the targeted cells containing mutated genes. If this happens, healthy cells may be damaged, causing other illness or diseases such as cancer (Missouri School of Medicine, n.d.).

Also concerning to many is that such therapy is often prohibitively expensive. While much of this therapy still occurs within clinical trials that cover the cost for the patient, gene therapy on the open market can be extremely pricey, making it inaccessible for many people. For example, Zolgensma, a gene therapy to treat spinal muscular atrophy, is the most expensive medication in the United States, costing over $2.1 million for a course of treatment (McQueen, 2022).

While such risks are real, most predict that our growing ability to precisely target problematic genes will continue to minimize these concerns. When this is coupled with the fact that gene therapy will continue to become easier and cheaper, it's easy to see why many believe we will see an exponential increase in the use of preventative and restorative somatic gene therapy of the types we're discussing over the next decades.

Moving from technical or functional risks to ethical and specifically religious concerns, while most are grateful for the role somatic gene therapy will continue to play in preventing disease and restoring us to normal health, both religious and nonreligious individuals who are opposed to germline gene editing – modifications that are inheritable – fear that allowing the editing of somatic (nonreproductive) cells to continue unchecked will open the door more widely and quickly to germline editing (the editing of reproductive cells).

Also, from a religious perspective, some believe that we are at this point really starting to "play God." This argument comes in various forms. For some, it's simply the vague feeling of uneasiness around our ability to manipulate God's creation to this extent. For others, something more specific is meant. For example, some who believe that there is a divine purpose for all we experience, including the pain and suffering we experience, feel that this sort of genetic manipulation for what we have decided are good ends is going too far – is playing God in ways we shouldn't.

For others, there is a concern that such activity is an attempt to abort God's plan for the restoration of creation. As a result of human rebellion against God, death entered the world and humanity's "genetic make-up and that of the rest of creation began a change toward demise. In some instances, genetic engineering could be seen as an attempt to undo this result of sin called the 'curse'." For us to go too far in an attempt to "restore things to an even better state" may interfere with the plans God has for doing so. Of course, other religious individuals argue that there is no reason to believe that our ability to intervene genetically is not, in fact, part of this divine restorative plan (Questions, n.d.).

Gene therapy is considered preventative or restorative when it restores a person to a healthy state. Accordingly, the potential impact of preventative/restorative somatic gene therapy is not limited to what we have been discussing to this point, which might be labelled diseases and conditions related to our "physical/bodily health." There are diseases and abnormal conditions such as depression, psychiatric disorders, and abusive and addictive traits related to our "psychological/ mental health." We now know that there are genetic factors in many of these diseases and abnormal conditions. Should preventative and restorative somatic gene therapy be used to treat these types of diseases/conditions/traits?

Not surprisingly, significant ethical, social, and legal issues come into play at this point. Assuming we can modify a person's genetic makeup to impact such "psychological/mental health" conditions, we must first clearly specify exactly what it is we are trying to accomplish. The goal of gene therapy is to return diseased or damaged cells to their normal state, and we have a fairly good idea of what that means in relation to cells in our "physical bodies."

What, though, counts as "normal" in relation to conditions such as chronic depression or harmful addictive tendencies if we actually come to the point where we can permanently address such conditions genetically? Do we want to genetically modify individuals so they no longer find themselves depressed or anxious or acting compulsively? If not, which I'm assuming is the case, where then do we draw the line? We might decide we want to allow individuals to experience depressive states (be very sad) or social anxiety or compulsive desires but not to the extent that the conditions are debilitating. Where is that line to be drawn and who decides?

Assuming we have the technology to draw that line at various places, do we require informed consent before such changes are implemented? However, if individuals are suffering the debilitating effects of such conditions, can they really give informed consent? Should friends and family with the power of attorney or medical experts be allowed to make such decisions? Should parents give informed consent for children? Should we allow such modifications to be advertised by for-profit companies, or would such genetic therapy need to remain more regulated?

It doesn't follow from the fact that there are at present no clear answers to such questions that treating debilitating psychological/mental conditions genetically should not be allowed by law or that such treatment is ethically abhorrent. It does demonstrate, though, that the technology (even in theory) is running ahead of our thoughtful consideration of its impact.

It is important to keep in mind here, it has been argued, that some will feel compelled to use such "restorative techniques," regardless of where the line is drawn, and even if they have concerns about the inherent value or related ethics. Individuals do not exist in social vacuums. Students are judged by how they do relative to their peers. If most students in a class have been genetically modified to a certain standard of normalcy, then not having your child genetically restored to the new "normal" will place your child at a disadvantage. The same could also hold in relation to individuals in the workplace. If most employees have been genetically restored to "normal" condition, those who have not will be at a disadvantage.

Moreover, it must be mentioned in concluding our discussion of preventative or restorative somatic genetic engineering that some will view such therapy in many of its forms as discrimination against persons with disabilities. Few will deny that some people who have physically, mentally, or emotionally disabling conditions are so, in part, as the result of genetic factors. In fact, most will acknowledge that by removing genetic disorders, and the resulting disabilities, we will have removed one of the sources of discrimination and inequality faced in society by individuals with these disabling conditions.

However, as some see it, the implicit assumption in using preventative or restorative genetic engineering is that people disabled through genetic factors need to be treated and made normal. And this, itself, some maintain, can be a form of discrimination.

A religious variant of this line of reasoning states that while helping those in need is indeed a worthy goal, we must be careful not unintentionally to forget that "God wants us to treat all as worthy and equal" apart from any disabling conditions.

4.2 Somatic Human Genetic Editing: Enhancements

As stated earlier, somatic genetic engineering is not limited to prevention or restoration. It could also be used to enhance humans. The goal here would not simply be to return some aspect of a person with diseased or damaged cells to a "normal" or "healthy" state. The goal would be to increase an ability or function beyond that which is "normal" or "healthy" for the person. Of course, we have many examples of nongenetic ways of increasing abilities or functions above that which is "normal." We have available to us, for instance, various forms of exercise and drugs that can impact our body shape, size, and stamina, and supplements to enhance memory. In one sense, gene augmentation would be just one additional means of acquiring desired enhancements. However, while all of the other means of enhancement noted are temporary, somatic genetic enhancements would be more permanent for the person receiving the treatment.

We aren't there yet. "The ability to enhance complex traits lies some distance in the future. Complex physical and mental traits, skills, and talents are mediated by more than one gene, by gene-gene interactions, and by gene-environment interactions ... and even if geneticists come to understand all this, they must still perfect technologies for replacing genes and for ratcheting gene expression up and down" (Lagay, 2000).

However, given the documented amount of effort and money expended by individuals to modify physical characteristics and mental faculties through nongenetic avenues, there is no doubt that there will be increasing interest in using genetic editing to make such changes. When we add to this the speed at which advances in genetic engineering are being made, it seems prudent that we begin to consider seriously the ethical and social implications of somatic genetic enhancement.

Not surprisingly, we also encounter here an enhancement variation of the argument that not to use genetic engineering to modify children or even adults when the majority of others are doing so is to place them at a social, psychological, and economic disadvantage. One interesting version is the following:

> One thing to consider with a technology like gene editing is that it affects more people than just the individual whose genes have been edited – and in some cases, those with edited genes could be unfairly better off than those who haven't had their genes enhanced. For example, if it were possible to enhance genes to improve facial symmetry or make a person more confident, it might mean these people are more likely to find employment in a competitive market, compared to those who haven't had their genes edited for these characteristics (Johnson, 2019).

Others disagree. Even if we assume that those who have not been enhanced will miss out on opportunities or be made to feel inferior or less loved for not doing so if such enhancement is widespread, this should not be viewed as a reason to support enhancement. It should, rather, be seen as a reason to prohibit somatic enhancement genetic editing.

Finally, many of the concerns noted in relation to preventative or restorative somatic genetic modification apply to genetic enhancement. For instance, the same risk and cost factors are present.

The problem of informed consent, especially as it relates to children, also remains and is amplified. We discussed before the right of a parent to decide whether to return a child to normalcy without the child's consent. However, while it seems that many children would thank their parents for restoring them to genetic normalcy (however it's defined), it isn't at all clear that a child should feel gratitude for an enhancement that the parents, not the child, have chosen, even if we add the debatable assumption that the enhancement was chosen only with the best interest of the child in mind.

4.3 Cloning: The Duplication of Human Genes

As noted earlier, while genetic engineering in its most literal sense is the altering of DNA within a gene to change the makeup of an organism, we are using a broader understanding of genetic engineering that includes the duplication of human genes (cloning).

In its most relevant basic somatic form, cloning involves (1) extracting an unfertilized egg from a donor female, (2) removing the nucleus (and thus DNA) from that egg, (3) inserting the nucleus (and DNA) from a somatic cell – for example, a skin cell – of a male or female cell donor into the egg from which the nucleus has been removed, (4) stimulating the now nucleated egg to develop into an embryo with the same genes (DNA) as the cell donor, and then (5) inserting the embryo with the DNA of the cell donor into the uterus of the female who will give birth to a genetic copy of the cell donor (Study.com, 2022).

Since the successful cloning of a sheep (Dolly) in 1996, we have cloned (produced identical genetic copies of) more than twenty types of animals – for example, dogs, cats, fish, sheep, goats, and monkeys. As we are now focusing on human genetics, I won't discuss what some see as the obvious benefits of animal cloning – which range from the cloning of superior animals for food production to the revival of extinct species to the ability to have a genetic copy of a favorite pet that has died.

While no humans have been verifiably cloned to date, the alleged benefits and concerns of doing so have been discussed since the birth of Dolly in 1996. I'll note here just one "benefit" often discussed: cloning as an option for producing children for infertile and same-sex couples. By inserting the cell nucleus from one of the partners into an enucleated egg that is then induced to the embryo stage before being implanted in the womb of the female partner or another female, the baby born would be a genetic twin of the cell donor. If we grant that the baby would no more be the *same person* as the cell donor than are identical twins, some see this as a viable option (assuming the procedures could be done safely).

Others, though, see human cloning as problematic apart from safety concerns. These concerns include the strong potential "black market" for selling clones of famous people, the potential for organizations/governments to clone groups of people physiologically/psychologically suited for certain tasks, and the potential harm to parents and/or children in parenting a genetic copy of themselves. And, not surprisingly, the charge of "playing God" receives more intense attention here.

While the cloning of a person is not yet a reality, therapeutic human cloning is very much a research interest for many (National Human Genome Research Institute, n.d.). The key building blocks for therapeutic human cloning are stem cells. Most cells in the body are associated with a specific, specialized function. They are, for example, brain, blood, or muscle cells, and they divide into daughter cells with the same function. Stem cells have no preset specialized function but can develop into cells with specialized functions.

Therapeutic human cloning is a specialized form of stem cell therapy using cells (and thus DNA) extracted from the person receiving the therapy. As is the case with full organism cloning, the nucleus (and thus DNA) from a somatic cell provided by a cell donor is inserted into an enucleated egg that is induced to grow to the embryo stage. However, unlike what occurs with full organism cloning, the embryo is not implanted into a birthing womb. Rather, embryonic stem cells with the DNA of the cell donor are extracted from the embryo. One option, which is already a reality, is then to turn these stem cells into specific types of cells that can be used to "fight some types of cancer and blood-related diseases, such as leukemia, lymphoma, neuroblastoma and multiple myeloma" (Goodyear Chiropractic, 2019). Another goal is to induce these stem cells to become tissue or organs – for example, skin tissue, a liver, or kidney. Since any tissue or organ formed in this fashion will have the same DNA of the cell donor, the tissue or organ will not be rejected by the donor's immune system if used to treat the cell donor.

Few find the goal of therapeutic cloning (or stem cell therapy) troubling, though there is one key ethical concern for some. While it is possible to acquire stem cells in various ways, the most common and effective way at present is by extracting stem cells from embryos. However, regardless of whether the stem cells extracted from an embryo are to be induced to treat the person whose nucleus is in the stem cell or not, an embryo is destroyed. As has been repeatedly noted, many religious (and some nonreligious) individuals believe that because each human embryo is a distinct human substance in the fullest sense, we should oppose procedures in medicine that involve their destruction. For some, this opposition is only at the "ethical" level in the sense that the goal is to convince others that they ought not end the life of an embryo. For others, this opposition moves to the "legal" level in the sense that their goal is to pass laws that make it a punishable crime to end the life of an embryo.

5 Genetics and Human Reproduction

As stated earlier, we are using a broader definition of genetic engineering that includes the increasing use of "genetic information" to make decisions about conception and prenatal intervention. What follows is a brief overview of the ways in which genetic information is relevant to these aspects of the childbearing process.

5.1 Preconception Testing and Counseling

Preconception counseling is increasingly being used by couples (or individuals) who desire or are considering having a baby. Genetic counselors, who have often been trained in genetics, medicine, and psychology, focus on genetic risk factor assessment. They review the family and medical history of the couple (or individual) to determine the chances of the baby being born with a myriad of problematic conditions, including chronic illnesses such as heart disease or diabetes and gene disorders such as muscular dystrophy, cystic fibrosis, sickle cell disease, and Fragile X syndrome, and then explain "the medical, emotional and familial implications of genetic disease" to the couple/individual. The goal of such counseling is not to influence the couple's decisions but rather to help the couple make informed choices about proceeding with attempted pregnancy (UK Health System, n.d.).

If such counseling indicates even the possibility of genetic disorders, one option discussed is carrier genetic screening. A sample of blood, saliva, or tissue from the inside of the cheek of one or both partners is tested to determine the presence of DNA linked to genetic disorders. Standard screening tests check for the disorders already mentioned, and expanded genetic carrier screening can now also detect hundreds of additional disorders. The goal here also is to provide "individuals/couples with information to assist them in understanding their reproductive risk for disease, family planning, considering reproductive options that align with their personal values and circumstances, and optimizing the opportunity to achieve a healthy pregnancy" (Sigma Repository, 2021).

For some of those whose testing indicates significant genetic risks, one option is to decide not to attempt to have biological children – to choose to remain childless. Others might choose to adopt. Still others might explore working with a fertility clinic to procure donor sperm/and or eggs that have been screened for genetic risks, with the resultant embryo implanted in the womb of the female desiring to have children or in a surrogate mother.

5.2 Preimplantation Genetic Testing

Yet another viable option, though, for those couples facing the possibility of significant genetic risks but wanting to have biological children is to utilize preimplantation genetic testing (PGT). The first step is for the couple to use the in vitro fertilization process to obtain embryos for testing. More specifically, eggs are extracted from the woman and fertilized with sperm from the man in a lab. When the fertilized eggs (embryos) reach a certain stage, some cells are taken and genetically analyzed for signs of genetic disorders of the type we have been discussing plus genetic abnormalities which can cause pregnancy loss and birth defects. Parents can then decide to not implant any embryos in the mother's womb or to implant only those embryos, if any, that don't appear to have genetic disorders or other abnormalities (Fertility Center, n.d.).

While there is still no guarantee that implanted embryos will result in a live birth or that the baby, when born, will not have any health concerns, this process does remove much of the anxiety that accompanies deciding to have a baby when genetic counseling predicted that there is significant chance a baby could be born with a specific undesirable genetic condition. The majority of fertility clinics currently offer PGT.

5.3 Prenatal Genetic Testing

For those couples who did not have genetic counseling or testing prior to pregnancy or had preconception counseling/testing but find themselves intentionally or unintentionally with a pregnancy, prenatal testing is available (Gardner, 2020). Such testing isn't focused only on genetic disorders. However, many of the types of testing available – for example, ultrasound, blood tests, chorionic villus (placenta tissue) sampling, and amniocentesis (the testing of amniotic fluid in the uterus) – can identify genetic disorders such as cystic fibrosis, sickle cell anemia, Tay-Sachs disease, and hemophilia; chromosomal disorders such as Down syndrome; and disorders such as spina bifida, which in most cases include both genetic and environmental factors (Spina bifida, n.d.)

Such testing has at least three primary purposes. It allows the couple (or a woman) who learns that there are concerning genetic conditions present to decide whether to terminate the pregnancy. For those who become aware of concerning genetic conditions but decide not to terminate the pregnancy, there is the opportunity to prepare psychologically and/or materially for the specific challenges they will face. For example, if the couple learns that the baby will be born with spina bifida, they can access the medical equipment needed and/or join a spina bifida support group. Finally, it allows for the treatment of an increasing number of problems before birth – for example, congenital diaphragmatic hernia, fetal anemia, and spina bifida. In some cases, treatment in the womb has a better result than treatment after birth.

5.4 Genetics and Human Reproduction: Concerns

While the benefits of accessing these gene-related preconception and postconception options have already been noted, concerns have been raised in relation to each.

Since preconception counseling and testing either help a couple or individual predict the likelihood of having a baby with genetic disorders *before a pregnancy*, concerns related to the termination of pregnancies do not arise here. However, other concerns remain. First, neither genetic counseling nor testing is 100 percent accurate. Actually being tested for carrying a faulty gene is, of course, more accurate than predicting this might be so on the basis of family history. There always remains, though, the possibility that the test will indicate there are genetic problems when there actually aren't and vice versa. Or, even if there are genetic problems, we will often "not be able to tell if they'll show symptoms of the disorder, how severe it will be, or if they'll get worse over time" (DerSarkissian, 2022). Such ambiguity can produce stress for the couple trying to make the "right choice" based on evidence.

Furthermore, reviewing family histories does not occur in a socio-psychological vacuum. Accessing information about what relatives have known and the choices they have made through the review of family medical histories can result in judgment and, at times, the disruption of extended-family dynamics.

Preimplantation genetic testing raises a number of concerns. Those religious and nonreligious individuals who believe that human life (of the type protected by law) begins at conception find this procedure ethically and/or legally unacceptable at two points. First, the required IVF process normally involves discarding fertilized eggs that haven't developed properly (are not viable) or storing fertilized eggs that many never be implanted in a womb. Second, the scanning of the fertilized eggs for genetic disorders frequently results in the discarding of embryos that evidence the genetic disorder the couple is trying to avoid. A related religious criticism is that this process treats a human as a commodity rather than an autonomous human life made in God's image.

Also, the cost of IVF is $10,000–15,000 per cycle, with insurance seldom covering the full, if any of the, cost. The average cost when such testing is added to the initial IVF cost is $17,000–25,000. This makes the process inaccessible to many and thus raises justice concerns related to equitable access.

Not surprisingly, prenatal (during pregnancy) testing faces some of the same concerns as preimplantation genetic testing. The main concern to some, especially those who are religious, is that such testing increases the likelihood of abortion. Other critics focus on the fact that testing can be inaccurate. Still others point out that access to such testing is often in direct proportion to a couple's (person's) socioeconomic status.

In response to the fact that we can now correct some problems in utero that cannot be corrected to the same extent after birth, some argue that we should simply accept and love the child we receive rather than trying to design the child we want. The counterargument is that while we can and should love a child facing challenges – for example, we can and should love a child with an arm that is dysfunctional because a bad break was never treated properly – it doesn't follow that we shouldn't do what we can to avoid those challenges – for example, that we should not treat a broken arm when we can.

A related concern is the explicit or implicit judgment those who agree to be tested can face, especially if results uncover problems. If a couple/woman decides to terminate the pregnancy, they will be judged by those who believe abortion is wrong, while if the couple/woman decides to continue the pregnancy, they will be judged for knowingly bringing a child with such problems into our world.

Finally, in relation to all forms of acquiring genetic information and subsequent action, for some who believe in a supreme being who controls earthly affairs or can intervene as needed, to engage in any of this activity evidences a lack of faith.

6 Germline Human Genetic Editing

We now come to the most controversial aspect of human genetic engineering: the genetic modification of germline (reproductive) cells. Let's review again how germline (reproductive cell) editing differs from somatic (nonreproductive) cell editing. Somatic therapy targets genes in a large number of specific types of cells (e.g., blood cells) while germline therapy targets only sperm, eggs, or early stage embryos. The edited gene in somatic therapy is only contained in the target cell (and subsequent daughter cells), with no other types of cells affected. The edited gene in germline therapy is copied into all new reproductive cells, including all sperm or egg cells. Any changes from somatic therapy are limited to the individual being treated. Any change from germline therapy is passed on to future generations (Bergman, 2019).

Why has germline gene editing received so much attention? We hear constantly about technological advances that will have a significant impact on humanity. We are told that the next generation of artificial intelligent "machines" with self-awareness will transform manufacturing and give us everything from safe, reliable self-driving vehicles to personalized nursing assistants. Internet enhancements coming soon, we hear, will transform data collection, storage, and accessibility in ways that will transform business, education, and leisure time, and do so in ways that will protect privacy (reduce hacking). We can 3D print with almost any material now – for example, plastic, metal, powder, concrete, and liquid – and produce everything from manufacturing machines to guns to houses. Improved printing techniques, we are told, will enable us to revolutionize manufacturing and create more and more highly useful personalized items on demand.

In some ways, germline (reproductive) genetic engineering is just like other world-transforming technologies: all have the potential to transform our world in ways that will be passed on to future generations. The key difference is that while the other technologies will transform the world in which our offspring will live, germline human genetic engineering has the potential to change profoundly our offspring themselves – that is, to change the humans who will be living in a world transformed by other technologies. It was in relation to the potential use of CRISPR to this end – namely, its ability to edit reproductive cells – that Jennifer Doudna has stated, as mentioned before, that the fact that CRISPR has "the power to control our species' genetic future is awesome and terrifying."

The potential genetic changes to humans, we've seen, fit into two basic categories: preventative changes that would remove undesirable genetic factors and enhancement changes that would add desirable genetic factors.

Germline gene-editing is still in the research stage. At present, preventative germline research is being done with the hope of eventually eliminating, or making people much less susceptible to, for example, HIV, hepatitis, herpes, inherited eye diseases, neurodegenerative conditions such as Alzheimer's disease and Huntington's disease, cystic fibrosis, muscular dystrophy, various forms of cancer, Down syndrome, genetic high cholesterol traits, genetic obesity traits, genetic substance abuse disorder, and even genetic baldness. Some even see preventative germline gene editing as a way of addressing mental illnesses, and possibly psychiatric disorders (Dalechek, 2021).

Obvious enhancements that are or will be possible soon include increased strength and modified body shape and height. There is also increasing discussion about the implications of germline gene editing for personality traits, which could include genetically predisposing individuals to be "friendly" or have a positive outlook on life, intelligence, and even economic behavior. Or to state this important point differently, the power of the germline enhancement technology currently under development now opens the real possibility that in the next two or three decades, people may have the option to enhance "themselves and their children in ways that, up to now, have existed largely in the minds of science fiction writers and creators of comic book superheroes" (Pew Research Center, 2016b).

6.1 Germline Editing and Gene Drives

However, since each person passes on only half of the needed chromosomes to offspring, doesn't that mean that any germline genetic changes in a given individual, be they preventative/restorative or enhancing in nature, might not manifest themselves significantly in future generations in the short term?

Perhaps not. Scientists are now working on what are called gene drives, which are tools that greatly increase the chance a certain gene is passed on to an organism's offspring. To be more specific, "gene drives work by ensuring that a higher proportion of an organism's offspring inherit a certain 'selfish' gene than would happen by chance, allowing a mutation or foreign gene to spread quickly through a population" (Callaway, 2018). Or stated differently yet, gene drives "dramatically increase the likelihood that a particular suite of genes will be passed onto the next generation, allowing the genes to rapidly spread through a population and override natural selection" (Coffey, 2020).

6.2 Preventative and Restorative Germline Genetic Editing: Benefits and Concerns

Let's consider first the proposed benefits and concerns related to preventative/ restorative germline gene editing. The key benefit of preventative/restorative somatic germline editing – that such editing has the potential to "cure" diseases and undesired conditions permanently for an individual – remains. However, unlike what is the case with preventative/restorative somatic gene editing, germline gene editing does not just "cure" the person undergoing the therapy. The person will also not pass on the genetic disease or undesired condition to their offspring.

One area of preventative germline gene editing research viewed positively by some focuses on delaying or stopping ageing. Even apart from the diseases that cause death, bodily systems currently simply slow down and wear out. "Cardiovascular disease (strongly age-related) is emerging as the biggest cause of death in the developing world. Ageing kills 30 million every year . . . age-related diseases, such as heart disease or cancer, are really the symptoms of an underlying disease: ageing" (Savulescu, 2015). If we used gene editing to not only help individuals facing these symptoms but to help eliminate or reduce the underlying causes in a way that can be passed on to future generations, it's possible there would be "humans living twice as long, or perhaps even hundreds of years, without loss of memory, frailty or impotence" (Savulescu, 2015).

Of course, to extend lifespans would bring with it the possibility of over-population or lack of resources to make life meaningful or enjoyable. However, the fact that extending life might bring with it hardships hasn't stopped us in the past from using technology to extend life, so it's not clear such potential hardships would or should stop us now, especially since the solution to such problems is less what can be done than the political will to do it.

We also encounter here a version of the comparative fairness argument used to support somatic preventative editing. We live in a world in which our ability to access fully the personal, social, educational, and economic benefits available requires that we have comparable physical and mental capacities. Accordingly, not to have your children undergo the preventative or restorative editing necessary to ensure to the extent possible that your children will throughout their lives be on a level playing field is to place your children both now and later at a social, psychological, and material disadvantage.

Some of the concerns noted in our consideration of preventative/restorative somatic gene editing remain but often with a (slightly) different focus.

The prohibitive expense of gene editing that threatens to exacerbate the gulf between the haves and have-nots is relevant to both somatic and germline editing. Since change from somatic gene editing is limited to the individual being treated while change from germline gene editing is passed on to future generations, it may be true in some cases that germline editing, unlike somatic editing, won't require the ongoing cost of the genetic "cure" in future generations. However, even the initial cost would be prohibitive for many so such editing still has the potential to lead to the emergence of "genetic castes" (Genetics & Society, 2006).

The difficulty of determining what it means to return a person to psychological/mental health is significant in both somatic and germline editing but is further complicated in germline editing by the fact that decisions made for this generation will be carried on into future generations, as would also be the case with respect to the difficult question of if/when returning a person to a "normal" state is discriminatory.

Preventative germline gene editing also carries with it a number of the technical risks noted in relation to somatic gene editing. However, some maintain that inheritable genetic modification for prevention/restoration constitutes a new level of unsafe human experimentation since it is impossible now to anticipate fully the ongoing effects of germline gene editing (Genetics & Society, 2006). However, while many will agree this is the case today, not everyone agrees that this will be the case in the not-too-distant future.

6.3 Enhancement Germline Genetic Editing: Benefits and Concerns

As the starting point to our discussion of the proposed benefits and concerns related to enhancement germline gene editing, I want to document and briefly discuss the one known case of actual human editing of this type. In early 2018, a Chinese team led by scientist He Jiankui genetically modified a particular gene in twin girls during their embryonic development using CRISPR. This was followed by seemingly healthy births in late 2018.

The goal was to make the girls (and their descendants) immune to HIV, the virus that causes AIDS. This aspect is probably best considered an example of preventative germline gene editing. However, some research indicates "that the same alteration introduced into the girls' DNA . . . not only makes mice smarter but also improves human brain recovery after stroke," and may lead to increased cognition and improved memory that could in humans, in turn, "be linked to greater success in school." If this did in fact occur, then while the ability of the brain to recover more successfully after a stroke would still be a restorative change, the heightened cognition and improved memory would be examples of human germline enhancement (Regalodo, 2019).

When the research was presented at a conference on human genome editing soon after the births, there was almost universal condemnation of this act, even within the scientific community. Dr. He and two of his research collaborators were indicted and found guilty of unethical behavior by Chinese authorities. Dr. He was sentenced to three years in prison and his collaborators sentenced to eighteen months each.

As of October 2020, seventy-five countries prohibit the use of genetically modified in vitro embryos to initiate a pregnancy (heritable genome editing). Five of these seventy-five countries provide exceptions to their prohibitions, while no country "explicitly permits heritable human genome editing" (Qaiser, 2020).

Furthermore, many in the scientific community agree that "a full set of laws, regulations along with the guidelines should be formulated to penalize genome-editing behaviors . . . more effective and binding mechanisms should be con-structed and implemented among different countries . . . and a collaborative network should be strengthened for better global registry and surveillance of human genome-editing technologies and research" (Lui, 2020).

In short, we see that most at present believe we should not be engaging in the germline editing of actual humans, even in controlled clinical trials. However, not everyone agrees. A pragmatic argument in favor of continuing approved and monitored enhancement germline research focuses on the inevitability of enhancement editing, once the technology is in place. "Inheritable genetic modification will occur even if banned, because demand will be strong and people will be willing to pay. Rather than encourage black markets and likely abuses, we should legalize the practice so that it can be safely regulated" (Genetics & Society, 2006).

In response, others counter that this "legalize because inevitable" line of reasoning is based on a faulty assumption: that whatever can't be stopped should be allowed in a manner that is fair and just for all. There are many things we can't stop to which we obviously don't and ought not apply this principle – for example, abuse and tax evasion. Our goal in such cases, rather, is to create laws and regulations to minimize these activities. The same should be applied here.

We also find here a version of the argument that it's unfair to our children not to take advantage of the genetic modification available. Enhancing germline editing could help individuals avoid some of the worst inequities that reproduction passes on now. "The biological lottery – i.e. nature – has no mind to fairness. Some are born gifted and talented, others with short painful lives or severe disabilities. While we may worry about the creation of a genetic masterclass, we should also be concerned about those who draw the short genetic straw" now (Savulescu, 2015). If germline genetic editing could make the playing field more level, this would only be just.

Others disagree, especially when this line of reasoning is applied to inheritable traits. Given that we always live in a social-economic-political context that is not shaped by genetic factors alone, we will never be in the position to determine that the physical/mental/emotional traits we have decided to pass on to level the playing field are, in fact, the traits or characteristics that will best enable individuals to compete on a level playing field in the actual sociopolitical-economic environments in which they find themselves in the future.

In addition, some of the key concerns with somatic enhancement become even more significant when raised in relation to germline enhancement. One is the problem of informed consent. We noted that it isn't at all clear that a child should feel gratitude for a somatic enhancement that the parents, not the child, have chosen, even if we add the debatable assumption that the enhancement was chosen only with the best interest of the child in mind. However, with germline enhancement, parents aren't just deciding that an enhancement is best for their child. They are deciding what is best for the offspring of their child for generations to come. Or stated differently, the worry here is "that it is impossible to obtain informed consent for germline therapy because the patients affected by the edits are the embryo and future generations" (Civilsdaily, 2019).

Of course, it might be argued that parents in the future can "re-modify" these enhancements if desired. This, though, raises a new concern. We know that everything from favorite names to favorite car colors to the most desirable body types change significantly in cultures over time. If/when we have the technology not only to enhance, but to re-enhance the size, shape, and even personality permanently in the manner we think "best," it isn't at all unreasonable to think that enhanced individuals will become dated by the decade or generation in which certain traits were popular.

Another key somatic enhancement concern that carries over is the risk of harmful or unintended side effects on our physical well-being. With somatic enhancement, any such harm is limited primarily to the person whose cells were edited. With germline enhancement, harm is passed on to offspring. For instance, it's been argued that germline enhancements could lead to pervasive, lasting innate immunity problems. "In a genetic supermarket some immune system genes may be more desirable than others, as they provide protection against the likeliest disease threats. However, if many parents pick the same immune system genes for their children, their combined actions may reduce population level immunodiversity, and this could make everyone worse off" both now and in the future (Gynyell & Douglas, 2014).

The same argument has been made in relation to cognitive traits. "Some cognition-related genes may be very popular in an unregulated genetic supermarket. However, the combined action of many parents choosing these genes for their children may reduce valuable types of cognitive diversity and make everyone worse off" both now and in the future (Gynyell & Douglas, 2014).

Others see the very real risk that enhancing children will cause parents to place unrealistic performance expectations on children – for instance, parents telling their children that they know they have the capacity to do better so poor performance must be the result of lack of effort. Such pressure, we know, negatively impacts the child's self-esteem and the parent-child relationship.

We also find here the reoccurring concern, especially for a number of religious individuals, that a necessary means to actualizing most of these enhancements eventuates in the destruction of human life. While noninheritable genetic enhancements involve the modification of somatic (nonreproductive) cells, inheritable genetic enhancement requires the modification of reproductive cells. To the extent that such enhancement involves the modification of embryos outside of the womb that came to be through in vitro fertilization, the likelihood that some embryos are destroyed or stored (and possibly never used) is high. For those who believe life begins at conception, this is unacceptable.

Finally, it's been my experience that while many religious individuals, as we have seen, are concerned that genetic engineering in any form is "playing God" – is tampering with God's creative plan for humanity in an unacceptable manner – it is at this point – where genetic changes are passed on to future generations – that many religious individuals don't just come to believe rationally but also to "feel deeply" that we have gone too far.

In concluding our overview of the lines of reasoning for and against enhancing germline editing, it's important to note that those who work or study in this area and have considered the pros and cons of such activity often come to very different conclusions. Some believe that when all the arguments are considered together, the case for allowing germline enhancement gene editing "is not compelling, and that the potential harms of doing so are immense" (Genetics & Society, 2006). Others who work in this area believe that the concerns are significant enough to merit serious social, legal, ethical consideration before deciding how to proceed. Still others maintain that such editing, "once proved safe and effective, should be allowed to cure genetic disease (and, indeed, that it is a moral imperative)," with concerns about enhancement "managed through policy and regulation" (Genome Research, 2017).

7 Genetic Engineering: How Ought We Think about All This?

To this point, I've shared with you (1) what I see as the current state of genetic engineering, especially as such engineering impacts humans and (2) what I see as the main lines of reasoning (arguments) offered in support of various perspectives on genetic engineering in general and various aspects in particular.

We'll turn now to the question of how we ought to think about all this, with special emphasis on how we should view the relationship between religious belief and human genetic engineering. Our discussion will be focused on three questions:

(1) How ought we in general assess the strength or weakness of the various lines of reasoning (arguments) presented?
(2) How ought we decide these issues for ourselves?
(3) How can we most productively engage in dialog with others about these issues?

Most of the lines of reasoning I've cited for and against genetic engineering in general or its specific forms are not formal arguments with explicitly stated premises and conclusions. It's difficult, accordingly, to apply some of the normal criteria for assessing arguments – for example validity and soundness for deductive arguments and the relevance and sufficiency of the evidence for inductive arguments. Moreover, I see no reason to attempt to turn these lines of reasoning into formal arguments for our purposes. An informal approach to assessment based on standard theories of ethical decision-making will, I believe, suffice.[2]

7.1 Approaches to Ethical Decision–Making

The ethical theories (approaches to ethical decision-making) we will be considering focus on how we *ought* to act. They give us ways of determining what is right or wrong.[3] As the basis for our discussion of my ought-related questions,

---

[2] While some distinguish between ethical and moral decision-making or ethical and moral choices, I'll be using the term "ethical" alone in both contexts.

[3] I want to acknowledge explicitly that there is an important approach to ethics – namely, virtue ethics – that does not focus primarily on how we *ought to act* but rather on the kind of person we *ought to be*. Moreover, there are a number of helpful discussions of virtue ethics and human genetic engineering available, for example *The Role of Virtue Ethics in Determining Acceptable Limits of Genetic Enhancement* (Karj, 2013: 109–116). However, focusing on theories concerned with how we ought to act offers us, I believe, the most productive way of assessing the

I want to outline what I see as the three most relevant approaches to ethical decision-making for our purposes, using a true story from World War II to illustrate the distinctions.

> As the Russian armies drove westward to meet the Americans and British at the Elbe, a Soviet patrol picked up a Mrs. Bergmeier foraging for food for her three children. Unable even to get word to the children, and without any clear reason for it, she was taken off to a prison camp in Ukraine. Her husband had been captured in the Bulge and taken to a POW camp in Wales.
>
> When he was returned to Berlin, he spent weeks and weeks rounding up his children; two (Ilse, twelve, and Paul, ten) were found in a detention school run by the Russians, and the oldest (Hans, fifteen) was found hiding in a cellar near the Alexander Platz. Their mother's whereabouts remained a mystery, but they never stopped searching. She, more than anything else, was needed to knit them as a family in that dire situation of hunger, chaos, and fear.
>
> Meanwhile, in the Ukraine, Mrs. Bergmeier learned through a sympathetic commandant that her husband and family were trying to keep together and find her. But the rules allowed them to release her for only two reasons: (1) illness needing medical facilities beyond the camp's, in which case she would be sent to a Soviet hospital elsewhere, and (2) pregnancy, in which case she would be returned to Germany as a liability. (Fletcher, 1966: 164–165)

Should Mrs. Bergmeier attempt to become pregnant? On what basis should she make her decision?

7.1.1 Consequence-Based Approaches

Consequentialism is an ends-based (teleological) approach to ethical decision-making that holds the right action to be that which brings about the best consequences overall; the means are not ethically relevant. Some consequence-based theories focus on the consequences for self, while other variants focus on the greatest good for the greatest number directly involved or the consequences of everyone acting in a certain way. For all consequence-based theories, the inherent ethical nature of the action isn't considered; what is right is determined by the consequences of the action alone.

If Mrs. Bergmeier uses this approach to ethical decision-making, she should not consider the ethical status of the action (attempting to get pregnant); she should consider only the projected consequence of getting pregnant. If she believes that becoming pregnant will produce the best consequences overall, then attempting to become pregnant is the right action. If she doesn't believe

---

comparative strengths and weaknesses of the various lines of reasoning I've presented and setting the stage for productive dialog with others.

becoming pregnant will produce the best consequences overall, then she should not do so.

Religious consequentialism holds the right action to be that which brings about what is understood in the religious tradition in question to be the best consequences overall, even if this requires not acting in accordance with some of the ethical principles in that tradition. Given that Mrs. Bergmeier is a Christian, if she believes that being with her children to care for them is the best consequence overall from a Christian perspective, then she should attempt to become pregnant to reunite with her family, even if the means of doing so requires her to break the biblical mandate against adultery. If she doesn't believe this is the best consequence overall from a Christian perspective, then she should not attempt to become pregnant.

7.1.2 Rule-Based Approaches

Rule-based (deontological) approaches to ethical decision-making maintain that the right action is that done in accordance with the relevant ethical principles. Consequences are not morally relevant. If Mrs. Bergmeier uses this approach to ethical decision-making, she should not consider the projected consequence of getting pregnant; she should consider only the ethical status of the action (attempting to get pregnant). If she believes that attempting to become pregnant is inconsistent with the relevant ethical principles, then she should not do so, even if she firmly believes that doing so will bring about the best consequences for her and her family.

Religious rule-based theories hold that we make the right decision when we act in accordance with the relevant religious principles. Even if the projected consequences of an action are considered inherently good by the religious tradition in question and adherents are encouraged to bring about these consequences when possible, adherents must avoid the temptation to bring about even good ends by any means. If the actions required to bring about these ends are prohibited by the relevant religious principles, it is not right to perform these actions. Accordingly, if Mrs. Bergmeier, as a Christian, believes that the key biblical principle here is that we are not to engage in sexual activity outside of marriage, then she ought not to attempt to become pregnant, even if she believes that returning to her family to care for her children is something that is of inherent value for Christians.

7.1.3 Intuition-Based Approaches

Intuition-based theories hold that what is right (making ethical judgments) is not determined solely by the rational consideration of the potential consequences or the application of relevant ethical principles arrived at through rational consideration. A key aspect of the decision-making process is based on what is directly apprehended – on what is self-evident. It must be noted, though, that there are two significantly different ways proponents of intuition-based theories can understand what it means for the right action to be self-evident.

One version, sometimes labeled "classical intuitionism," doesn't assume that the right answer in each case will be self-evident. Rather, classical intuitionists maintain that "basic [ethical] propositions are self-evident – that is, evident in and of themselves – and so can be known without the need of any argument" (Stratton-Lake, 2020). We then make ethical decisions by applying these principles to specific issues/situations at hand. We might, for instance, have the self-evident intuition "that all people are to be treated fairly, that it is wrong to intentionally harm an innocent person for no reason, or that all people are to be treated with dignity" and then use these self-evident ethical judgments as the basis for deciding what is right in a specific situation (Beard, 2020).

Mrs. Bergmeier, if a classical intuitionist, will not be making her decision on the basis of potential consequences or by identifying through rational consideration the relevant ethical principles and deducing from them the right action. The relevant ethical principles she should apply in this case will simply be self-evident to her. Religious intuitionists will sometimes add at this point that such principles are self-evident because we (including Mrs. Bergmeier) are made in God's image, and this carries with it an awareness of the basic ethical principles grounded in God's nature.

Understood in this fashion, classical intuitionism is actually a form of rule-based ethical decision-making, since in all rule-based approaches, the right action is determined by the application of the relevant ethical principles. What is unique in classical intuitionism is not the role that principles/rules play in decision-making. What is unique is the *source* of the ethical principles in question. In some rule-based variants, ethical principles are grounded in rational considerations. In other variants, including religious classical intuitionism, the ethical principles are grounded in God's moral nature. For nonreligious classical intuitionists, these principles are self-evident – we just "know" them to be true.

There is, though, another form of intuition-based ethical decision-making that does not involve the conscious application of self-evident ethical principles to a situation. This form of intuition-based ethical decision-making, which I will label "direct intuitionism," assumes that we can know certain ethical truths simply on the basis of experience, without the need for "conscious deliberation or any significant chain of inference" (Patterson, Rothstein, & Barbey, 2012). For these individuals, what is right (or wrong) in specific situations is what is directly sensed to be right (or wrong) in those situations.

Given this approach, Mrs. Bergmeier would not be making her decision by determining how the ethical rules of which she is self-evidently aware apply in her case. She would "simply" sense what is right or wrong and act accordingly. Another example would be those who tell us that various aspects of genetic engineering should be opposed because it just "feels" wrong.

Of course, to say that some actually use this method to make ethical decisions, which seems clearly to be the case, is not to say that any given person uses only this approach. Most who admit to using this approach at times would acknowledge that they at other times appeal to consequences and/or the rational application of ethical principles. This approach is most likely to be used when time constraints don't allow for conscious, rational consideration or when the interplay among all the factual and normative factors is too complex and/or leads to conflicting conclusions. Someone might, for example, use rational consideration rather than direct intuition when deciding whether it is right to lie to save a life or deciding if the cloning of a person is acceptable, since the key factors in these cases seem clear. But this same person might fall back on direct intuition when deciding whether somatic genetic editing is acceptable to reduce the likelihood of suffering from severe clinical depression since the relevant descriptive and normative factors are perceived as too complex in this case to offer a clear rational path forward.

Nor is maintaining that some at times rely on direct intuition to deny that the intuitions in question are often or always based on the unconscious application of implicit knowledge – for example, information, past experience, and/or general ethical principles – to which a person, perhaps unknowingly, has access. It is simply to maintain that "trusting your feeling" – your ethical sensibilities – is an acceptable (or only) option in certain contexts.

A religious version of direct intuitionism – that we need at times to turn directly to God for the answer – is utilized in at least three contexts. As will be discussed in greater detail later, some religious individuals acknowledge that religious ethical principles – for example the principle that we should never lie and the principle that we should save lives – sometimes conflict. It is perfectly justifiable in such cases, they maintain, to ask God to communicate to us directly the right course of action.

Second, there are religious individuals who believe, when considering a specific situation, that they have identified the relevant ethical principles but don't feel they (or others) are equipped to decide correctly how exactly these principles apply to the situation in question and turn directly to God for the correct application. For instance, someone might believe, when deciding whether genetic screening is acceptable, that the principles of helping those in need, causing no harm, and trusting God all apply but not have a clear sense of how these principles interplay in this context so turn to God for the answer.

Third, religious individuals who believe we should bring about the best consequences overall from a religious perspective don't always feel they are equipped to identify all the relevant consequences and determine how they should be correctly weighted. These individuals, too, sometimes turn to God directly for the "correct" response.

7.2 Ethical Decision-Making Approaches Applied to Genetic Engineering: Key Factors for Consideration

How does this categorization of approaches to ethical decision-making impact our current goal, which is to determine how best to assess the strength and/or weakness of lines of reasoning related to human genetic engineering in general and specific aspects in particular?

First, I want to note a way in which I believe this categorization is not helpful in this context. It might be tempting to maintain that how we as individuals assess these lines of reasoning will (or should) depend to a large extent on our own personal approach to ethical decision-making. If we are rule-based in our thinking, then our responses should be based on the application of the general or religious principles we believe most relevant in each case. If we are consequence-based in our thinking, then our ethical assessment of issues related to genetic engineering should be based on what we believe a cost/benefit analysis shows to produce the greatest net good in each case. If we are intuition-based in our decision-making, then our ethical assessment of these issues will either be based on what we deduce from self-evident principles or what just seems to us to be right in each case.

The problem here, as I see it, is that this reductionistic perspective is not reflective of the manner in which we normally make ethical decisions. Specifically, it's been my experience that almost no one utilizes just one of these approaches to ethical decision-making in all contexts. I've had the opportunity over the span of my teaching career to discuss ethical decision-making with well over 10,000 traditional undergraduate and graduate students and well over 10,000 working professionals from the fields of health care, business, social work, education, and religious ministry. What I discovered is that almost no one, religious or not, is solely rule-based, consequence-based, or intuition-based in relation to all issues. What I found, rather, is that the overwhelming majority acknowledged the value of all three ethical approaches (or ethical filters), which they normally utilize as needed and often in a specific order (whether they initially recognized this or not).

For most, issues to which they were to give an ethical response were first considered in relation to their rule-based filter, which at times settled the issue.

Let's consider a question we often discussed: whether capital punishment is justified in any situation. For those who believed (on religious or nonreligious grounds) that life-threatening force is never justified, the consequences and/or personal appeal of the practice of capital punishment rightly never came into play. The relevant rule determined that the practice must be considered unjustified in all cases.

When their rule-based filter did not settle the issue for many, their ends-based (consequence-based) filter often came into play. I often heard, for instance, that we need the practice of capital punishment in some cases because capital punishment is (can be) an effective deterrent for potential murderers or that capital punishment will at the very least keep convicted murderers from murdering or abusing individuals in the future (even if only in prison). On the other hand, some argued that capital punishment ought not be practiced because there is no evidence that it is, in fact, a deterrent.

For those whose consequence-based filter did not resolve the issue, their responses sometimes reflected an intuition-based approach. I don't find either the rule-based or consequent-based arguments compelling, they would say. Rather, capital punishment just seems right or wrong (or just seems compatible or incompatible with my faith) to me. Then there were some for which none of the three filters supplied an answer, so they simply remained unsure of their stance on this issue.

In short, to generalize the point for our purposes, while many of us might find ourselves favoring and utilizing one of these three approaches to ethical decision-making most often, it's my belief that to assume that we ought to analyze the lines of reasoning related to genetic engineering primarily by assessing them through the approach we tend to favor is inadequate because it is inconsistent with the way ethical decisions are normally made.

Furthermore, I don't believe it helpful to attempt to determine whether any given line of reasoning is, itself, best viewed as fully consequence-based, rule-based, or intuition-based. Some lines of reasoning fit primarily into one. Those lines of reasoning related to the impact of plant and animal genetic engineering on human well-being clearly fit primarily into the consequence-based category. However, as we will see, many, if not most, of the lines of reasoning we've encountered contain components from more than one of our ethical decision-making categories. That is, we'll see that the assessment of lines of reasoning that appear rule-based often necessitate consequence-based and/or intuition-based considerations, while the assessment of lines of reasoning that appear consequence-based often necessitate the consideration of ethical principles and/or ethical intuitions.

Accordingly, I feel that the best way to determine the strength and weakness of the lines of reasoning used to support challenges to genetic engineering in general and specific aspects in particular is to determine the extent to which consequence-based, rule-based, and/or intuition-based *components* are present and then assess the strength and/or weakness of these components before assessing the strength or weakness of the line of reasoning overall.

A key factor in assessing these components, and then lines of reasoning overall, is determining the extent to which the claims made are objective fact and/or personal, subjective opinion. For our purposes, an objective claim (statement, contention) is one based on evidence or factors that are, in principle, accessible to all and can be proved right or wrong by generally accepted criteria. As such, these are claims on which, in principle, equally knowledgeable and sincere individuals will not normally differ.

A subjective claim (statement, contention) is one based on evidence or factors that cannot, in principle, be validated (proved right or wrong) on the basis of generally accepted criteria. Accordingly, these are claims on which equally knowledgeable individuals can justifiably differ.

With all this in mind, we will turn to the identification and consideration of the key factors that make the application and assessment of these approaches to ethical decision-making, as they appear as components in lines of reasoning, so complex.

7.2.1 Key Factors Related to Consequence-Based Components

Let's turn first to the key factors that make the application and assessment of consequence-based components in lines of reasoning so complex. Since consequentialism is based on an assessment of the relevant consequences, the value (strength) of this approach to ethical decision-making increases or decreases in direct proportion to the comprehensiveness of the consequence-based scan. In some cases, identifying the relevant consequences is fairly straightforward. During World War II, some individuals hiding Jews in their homes were asked if they were doing so. The consequence of telling the truth would be probable death for those being hidden; the consequence of lying (successfully) would be that those hidden would not be found and put to death, while the consequences of not lying successfully would probably mean the death of those being hidden and the person(s) lying.

In most cases, though, to determine all or even most of the relevant positive and negative consequences of any action can be a daunting task. In Mrs. Bergmeier's case, there are significantly more possible consequences than her just being with her children again. For example, she needs to consider the impact of pregnancy on her own health and how that impact might affect her ability to care for her children if she is released. She also needs to consider what she might be facing if she becomes pregnant but isn't allowed to leave the camp; what she will do if she becomes pregnant, is allowed to return home, but her husband rejects her; and what the baby might face if it is ostracized by the family and/or community.

Such complexity becomes exacerbated when considering the possible consequences of gene editing activity. Many of the general lines of reasoning for and against genetic engineering are clearly consequence-based or have consequence-based aspects, focusing on specific actual or potential impact on humans. Some of these consequences are short-term; some are long-term. Other consequences are mainly technical; still others are psychosocial, religious, and/or economic. In relation to the various forms of somatic and germline gene editing, for instance, we need to consider not only the risks associated with the editing itself but also the short-term and long-term psycho-social (and for some religious) consequences of such activity for those undergoing treatment and for humanity in general.

Of course, it's unlikely in many cases that we will be able to identify all consequence-based factors, while it is likely that the consequence-based data we consider will change over time and with that our ethical perspective on the issues. However, at any point in time, the general principle holds: the value of the consideration of consequence-based factors increases in proportion to the comprehensiveness of the consequence-based scan.

Second, it's also necessary to assess in some way and to some extent the likelihood (probability) that the consequences identified will in fact occur. We routinely make consequence-based assessments of this sort in our daily lives. We all know it's possible that the lettuce we buy can cause botulism, that the tires on our cars can blow out with catastrophic effects when travelling at high speed, and that our heating and cooling systems can malfunction, even if properly maintained. We normally determine, though, based on objective data, that the probability of these negative consequences actually occurring is quite low so continue to buy lettuce, drive at high speeds, and use our heating/ cooling units (unless given some specific reason in a specific case not to do so).

However, in many situations, this sort of objective probability is not available when assessing consequence-based components of lines of reasoning. Let's again consider Mrs. Bergmeier's situation. Even if she does roughly know from past experience the likelihood that pregnancy will impact her health in a negative manner, it seems unlikely that she will have much past experience or any objective data to help her determine the probability of negative consequences on her health if she's pregnant but not allowed to leave, the probability that her husband and children will accept or reject her if she returns, or the probability of the child being ostracized.

Such complexity is obviously significant in relation to genetic engineering. The extent to which certain forms of genetic editing will have a negative, undesired impact on cells/human bodies will quite likely become clearer over time. However, the fact that we don't now have objective consensus on this question inserts a subjective element into our current ethical considerations. More specifically, while experts differ currently on the question of whether or at least the extent to which genetic editing is risky, the fact that we will likely be able to make a more objective determination in the future doesn't in any sense diminish the element of subjectivity in our current risk determination since we don't at present know whether more objective studies in the future will show the risk to increase or decrease.

It's even more difficult to see how we will in any objective manner be able to determine the probability of the short-term and long-term social, psychological, economic, and/or religious consequences (for some) of genetic engineering in many cases. For instance, when trying to determine the likelihood that germline genetic editing can increase the quality of life for humans, it's even doubtful that we will be able to reach any sort of objective consensus around what it means to have a higher or lower quality of life, which would be a prerequisite to determining in any objective sense whether germline gene editing would enhance or diminish the quality of life for those undergoing treatment or humanity in the future.

Moreover, even if we have identified the consequence-based factors and roughly assigned probabilities based on a projected future, we will still at times face the prioritization of conflicting or competing consequences. Sometimes this may not be a significant concern. Let's assume that saving the lives of innocent individuals by successfully lying is no more or less probable for a person than being caught lying unsuccessfully and killed. How is the person, if making a consequence-based decision, to decide? If the person is an egoistic consequentialist who judges consequences in terms of self, this person will probably choose not to lie, while if the person is a utilitarian consequentialist who judges consequences in terms of the greatest good for the greatest number, this person will probably choose to lie. In short, sometimes the type of consequentialism a person affirms will determine how competing consequences are prioritized.

However, we can imagine situations in which this is not the case. Let us assume that a person has good evidence that a powerful medication can successfully treat a very undesirable condition but also equally good evidence that taking the drug has very undesirable side effects or that a person has good evidence that a procedure will extend life but with diminished quality and that no consequence-based factors in either case tips the scale one way or the other when considering what is best for the person's own life or for the lives of others. It appears to me reasonable (and in keeping with what actually happens) to assume that subjective non-consequence-based value judgments – an intuitive sense of what's best – will often come into play in cases like this. This is also consistent with my prior claim that ethical decisions sometime pass through a person's ends-based, consequence-based filter to a more subjective (intuitive) level.

Such intuition-based value judgments seem to me especially likely in consequence-based considerations related to genetic engineering. Let's assume we are quite certain that various forms of the genetic engineering of animals will increase the amount of available food for those in need but equally certain that this will increase energy consumption in undesired ways. Or let's assume that when considering germline genetic editing to remove disease-related traits we all believe have no inherent value, we find ourselves convinced that such editing would be of value but also that our inability to make such editing accessible to all will only exacerbate the gulf between the privileged with power and money and those without. In both cases the final decision would, I believe, likely be based in part on a non-consequence-based, intuition-based value judgment.

To acknowledge this is the case is not to turn our ethical focus from consequences to the action that produced them. The focus remains on the consequences. I do believe, though, that in some (many) cases, non-consequence-based value judgments grounded in religious or nonreligious intuition will come into play when determining the ethical response to which the consequences are pointing us. If so, it's important to identify where such intuition-based value judgments do (or can) appear when considering the strength and weakness of predominately consequence-based components in lines of reasoning.

Finally, I don't think that the temptation to use consequence-based considerations to proof-text positions that are actually held for non-consequence-based or a limited set of consequence-based reasons can be overstated. When I talk with individuals about human genetic engineering, especially in a religious context, I find that many already possess a (strong) feeling or sense about whether such engineering is something that they should support, reject, or simply avoid thinking about seriously, a feeling often based on "horror" or "success" stories they've heard, what religious or nonreligious authority figures in their lives have told them, and/or simply a "gut level" reaction. Many, though, are more than happy to highlight "objective" consequence-based data to support the positions they already hold.

That is why I don't consider most formal or informal debates on human genetic engineering to be of value if the goal is to encourage decision-making based on the consideration of all the relevant factors. This is not to say that the debate format does not have value. It can help individuals clarify their thinking, better organize their thoughts, and improve their analytic skills. However, debate models of the type I'm discussing do not have as the primary goal to give those involved as participants or observers as comprehensive and neutral an understanding of the issues as possible so a thoughtful decision can be made. The goal of each participant, rather, is to win – to convince those listening that there are better reasons to affirm the position being set forth and defended than the position of their opponent. And a common strategy for doing so is to cite all the available data (reasons) for supporting the position while purposely not citing any counter-evidence and vice-versa.

This strategy is not limited to debates. The strategy of highlighting supportive evidence while avoiding the mention of counterevidence can occur in any educational, social, political, or religious setting, especially if a person has a religious or nonreligious reason for believing it important that others agree with the position being promoted or defended.

Or to generalize this point for assessment purposes related to genetic engineering, we need to consciously avoid the temptation to use consequence-based data to proof-text what we already believe to be the right answer. And when considering the consequence-based positions of others, we need always be asking what we are *not* being told that might be relevant.

Before turning to rule-based theories, I want to share the rest of Mrs. Bergmeier's story and make a final comment.

> [Mrs. Bergmeier] turned things over in her mind and finally asked a friendly Volga German camp guard to impregnate her, which he did. Her condition being medically verified, she was sent back to Berlin and to her family. They welcomed her with open arms, even when she told them how she had managed her release. When the child was born, they loved him more than all the rest, on the view that little Dietrich had done more for them than anybody. (Fletcher, 1966: 165)

This story has, in fact, a happy ending. Things could, though, have turned out much differently for Mrs. Bergmeier. The commandant could have been lying to her for various reasons. Her family might not have accepted her or baby Dietrich. However, she didn't know what might occur when she made her initial choice. So citing what did happen as confirmation that she made the right choice cannot be used to justify her initial decision.

However, it's been my experience that this is exactly what is sometimes done. Individuals do sometimes judge whether a decision was right or wrong by what the consequences actually turned out to be. So I want to complete this section by offering a cautionary principle related to consequence-based considerations. While it's perfectly justifiable to utilize the information we have about the probable or actual consequences of a given course of action – for example, the probable or actual consequences of certain forms of genetic testing or gene editing – when making decisions, we need to guard against using information to which we didn't have access when a decision was made as a retroactive basis for a positive or negative assessment of that decision. For example, as we learn more about the probability of risk associated with certain forms of genetic editing, we will need to guard against using this information to judge retroactively the risk-related decisions made before this new information was available.

7.2.2 Key Factors Related to Rule-Based Components

Turning now to the key factors that make the application and assessment of rule-based components in lines of reasoning related to genetic engineering so complex, I want first to state that the ethical principles that are to guide right thinking in rule-based decision-making only have ethical standing to the extent that it can justifiably be maintained that the source in which these principles are grounded is an authoritative basis for ethical truth.

For religious individuals, the source of the normative ethical principles is normally God or the Divine, accessed via a religious text, a religious leader, or a religious intuition. For others, as already noted, the ethical principles are grounded in reason. The best-known and influential example is the ethical absolutism developed by Immanuel Kant, whose "categorical imperatives" – variations of the Golden Rule – were grounded in reason instead of divine authority (Britannica, 2020). Still others, as already noted (and will be discussed in greater detail later), believe ethical principles "are self-evident – that is, evident in and of themselves – and so can be known without the need of any rational argument."

The important question is obvious: Can any of these three stipulated sources of ethical principles be justifiably considered an authoritative basis for ethical truth? Unfortunately, the arguments on both sides of this question for all three sources are many and complex, with no clear consensus among philosophers, theologians, and others who think and write on this subject. I happen to believe, as I've argued elsewhere, that there exists no set of non-question-begging criteria by which it can be established objectively that the ethical authority of any of the sources in question must be affirmed or cannot justifiably be denied by all rational individuals (Basinger, 2020b). But that's not the point. The key point for our purposes is this: for anyone assessing rule-based components in lines of reasoning related to genetic engineering, these rule-based components will only be significant factors to the extent the sources in which the relevant ethical principles are grounded in what are considered authoritative sources.

Another key factor for consideration when assessing rule-based components in lines of reasoning is, as it was for consequence-based components, the extent to which the list of relevant ethical principles is comprehensive. The concern here is not just the difficulty of identifying all the relevant ethical principles. An additional, more significant difficulty is that among those who claim the same source for ethical principles, differing, even contradictory ethical principles sometimes emerge. Not all religious individuals who ground their ethical principles in the same religious texts believe that life begins at conception; the same is true for those who ground ethical truth in reason or intuition. Some with the same authoritative source for ethical truth maintain that knowingly bringing about the death of an innocent person is always wrong, while others make exceptions – for example, approving a drone strike to eliminate a terrorist when it's known innocent family members will likely also be killed or approving abortion when the mother's life is danger. Some who ground ethical truth in religious texts believe that tampering with God's creation is always wrong; other believe that the ability to "tamper" with God's creation is, itself, a gift from God; and still others maintain that such tampering is acceptable in some contexts but not in others.

Sometimes the basis for this tension is the distinction between "sins of commission" and "sins of omission." Assume that a person could have saved a drowning child but chose not to. Further assume that when criticized for failing to help, the person responded that she didn't *do* anything wrong – that the child did not drown because of any action on her part. The obvious response would be that we have a duty to help those in dire need to the extent we can, so failing to save the drowning child – an omission – is just as wrong as bringing it about by some action that the child is drowning – a commission.

Applied to our focus on genetic engineering, we must always, when assessing rule-based components in lines of reasoning, identify and consider not just those relevant ethical principles that speak to what it is right or wrong *to do* but also to those relevant principles that speak to what it is wrong *not to do*. For example, while rule-based components in lines of reasoning related to the ethics of editing somatic cells often focus primarily on rules that stipulate whether *engaging* in such editing is ethically right or wrong, we must also identify and consider those relevant ethical principles that speak to whether *not engaging* in such editing is right or wrong.

Even if we agree on which ethical principles are (or should be) included in rule-based lines of reasoning focused on genetic engineering, a related but distinct consideration is the meaning of the relevant principles. Many would agree, for instance, that the stipulation that we not "play God" – not go too far – can be a relevant ethical principle when responding to the question of whether various forms of genetic engineering are ethically acceptable. However, whether and, if so, to what extent "playing God" is relevant to our discussion of genetic engineering depends to a great extent on whether "playing God" is referring to any activity that intervenes in any natural bodily process (which would include Caesarean births and knee replacement), to any activity that will permanently alter a genetic aspect of persons for future generations, or to something in-between.

An important related example of ambiguous meaning in religious principles can be found in the common citing of the principle that it is unethical to engage in activity that runs counter to (is unjustifiably tampering with) God's plan for humanity. Theological determinists in various religious traditions maintain that God is all-controlling, even with respect to what we "freely" do. Not all that occurs may have inherent value for God. However, all that occurs is a necessary component in God's perfect creative plan (Basinger, 2013). If this is the case, then while we might debate whether genetic engineering is inherently desirable to God, we can rest assured that the fact that genetic engineering is possible and all that will eventuate as the result of such engineering in the future is part of God's plan.

On the other hand, freewill theists in various religious traditions maintain that although God could be all-controlling, God has chosen to grant us meaningful freedom, and in those situations where God allows the exercise of such freedom, what occurs may well not be in keeping with what God desires or believes best (Basinger, 2013). If this is the case, then whether what God desires to occur actually does occur in relation to genetic engineering is dependent significantly on whether we make the choices God would have us make. So that we identify and consider seriously the relevant religious principles becomes very significant.

Other examples could be given, but the general point should be clear. Since ethical/religious principles are often subject to significantly different meanings, an assessment of rule-based components requires that we be clear on the meaning intended in the line of reasoning in question.

Even if we have identified what we believe to be the relevant ethical principles and clarified their meaning, whether the religious principles in question are being applied appropriately needs to be considered. As a general rule, the extent to which the application of an ethical principle in a rule-based component is open to question is dependent on the extent to which this principle includes explicit reference to the action to which the principle is being applied. In Mrs. Bergmeier's situation, the religious principle normally noted – that adultery, defined as sexual intercourse outside of marriage, is wrong – includes explicit mention of the action she is contemplating. So the relevance of this principle is obvious.

Another example of the noncontroversial application of an ethical principle appears in the line of reasoning that states that preimplantation genetic embryo selection is wrong because it is incompatible with the ethical right to life of an embryo since the selection process requires in vitro fertilization that often does result in embryos being discarded.

At other times, the application of an ethical principle is only conditionally noncontroversial. Consider again the line of reasoning that states that genetic engineering is wrong because it inappropriately tampers with God's plan. The application of this principle, as we have seen, is only relevant if we assume that humans have the capacity to make free choices that are contrary to God's perfect plan.

In many other cases, though, the actions being ethically evaluated in a rule-based component in a line of reasoning aren't explicitly mentioned in the principles being referenced. We find nothing explicit noted about fixing faulty genes to restore health, modifying genes to enhance traits, or modifying the genetic structure of plants or animals to benefit humans in the purportedly relevant ethical principles that state we ought to help those in need or ought not tamper with God's plan (given any meaning). The alleged relevance of ethical principles in such cases is based on the additional belief (assumption) that the action being ethically "judged" by the ethical principles in question falls within the scope of the principle. The contention that the genetic engineering of plants and animals is ethically appropriate because we ought to do that which, on balance, helps humanity is based on the assumption that such engineering will impact humans in a manner that is, on balance, beneficial. The contention that we ought not to engage at present in human genetic engineering because we ought to avoid doing that which will subject humans to what is on balance long-term harm is based on the belief (assumption) that to engage in human genetic engineering at present carries with it a statistically meaningful probability that the resulting significant long-term harm will not be outweighed by any good. Likewise, the contention that we ought not to engage in germline human enhancement because it is likely to widen the gap between those with power and money and those without and to knowingly widen this gap is wrong is based on the belief (assumption) that enhancement will actually have this effect.

Two important points follow. First, all assumptions of this sort are open to challenge apart from an assessment of the ethical status of the principles in question, which means, to generalize, that when assessing any rule-based component in a line of reasoning based on principles that don't explicitly include the action under ethical evaluation, there are actually two points of challenge. We can challenge the ethical standing of the ethical principle itself (by challenging the ethical authority of the source) or challenge the assumption(s) that allegedly bring the action under the scope of the principle.

Second, such cases confirm the fact that lines of reasoning related to genetic engineering that appear rule-based sometimes contain consequence-based components. We can't by the consideration of any set of relevant rules alone determine whether the assumptions hold. In all these cases, consequence-based considerations – for example, the impact of genetic engineering on humans – are necessary to determine to what extent the action is under the scope of the principle, with these consequence-based considerations, themselves, being open to assessment in keeping with guidelines already noted for consequence-based components.

A final significant challenge for all who base ethical decision-making on the relevant ethical principles is, as briefly noted earlier, that the relevant ethical principles sometimes conflict. For instance, one variation of the principle of nonmaleficence states that those whose actions/activity directly affect humans – physicians, researchers, therapists – should do no harm while one variant of the principle of beneficence obligates those whose actions/activity directly affect humans to act in ways that will benefit those in need. However, acting in ways that will benefit those in need often carries with it the risk of harm. When a practitioner decides to continue or not continue to treat a patient in a way that could be of benefit given the risks, it's seldom the case that the practitioner has decided that one of the principles is no longer relevant. Rather, the relevant conflicting principles are being prioritized.

A helpful religious example is the decision-making process used by some religious individuals when deciding whether to hide Jews from the Nazis. They believed their faith taught both that they should never lie and that they should save the lives of innocent people when it is within their power to do so. Some decided that it was justifiable to lie to save lives; others didn't. In neither case was it determined that one of the principles was no longer true or relevant. The relevant conflicting principles were being prioritized differently.

Not surprisingly, when considering rule-based lines of reasoning in relation to somatic or germline genetic engineering, we often find explicit or implicit tensions (conflicts) between the duty to aid those in need (e.g., to help alleviate the pain and suffering by editing abnormal somatic cells to eliminate very undesirable traits for future generations) and the duty to minimize harm (e.g., not subject individuals to editing that can cause permanent harm or engage in activity that will widen the gap between those with power and money and all others.)

In some religious rule-based lines of reasoning, we don't encounter only the conflicts between the principles of nonmaleficence (do no harm) and beneficence (do good). We also find potential conflicts between these two principles and a sanctity of life principle: that every life has great value and should be treated with dignity and respect. This is clearly the case, for instance, when determining which principles should guide our ethical thinking in relation to preimplantation genetic screening or any form of germline editing that involves in vitro fertilization since this process normally results in the discarding of human embryos believed to have the right to life.

Proponents of rule-based approaches to ethical decision-making often acknowledge that the weighting and prioritizing of conflicting principles is a difficult task. Sometimes this prioritization is set by an organization. The National Commission of Human Subjects Protection states that when Institutional Review Board regulators encounter a conflict between informed consent and beneficence, "the regulations say that beneficence prevails when there is very little at stake with regard to self-determination" (Human Subjects Protection, n.d.).

Normally, though, especially in rule-based approaches to issues related to genetic engineering, prioritizations are not predetermined, and individuals are left to make the decision on their own. One option frequently practiced is to "evaluate the consequences of each option" and do that which will be most beneficial or least harmful. Another option is to do what intuitively feels right.

It must be noted here that some religious individuals who would have us follow God's rules ascribe to nonconflicting absolutism. That is, they believe that while there might appear on the surface to be conflicts between absolute ethical principles, this is actually not the case. If the ethical rules or principles are properly understood, there is never an actual conflict. For instance, a nonconflicting ethical absolutist would say that the rule stating that we should save innocent human life and the rule stating that we should not lie, when properly understood in context, would never actually be in conflict. The same would hold in Mrs. Bergmeier's case, where the claim would be that there is no actual conflict between the ethical mandate not to engage in "adultery" and the mandate to care for one's children.

However, as mentioned earlier, there are other religious individuals who would have us follow God's rules that acknowledge that absolute ethical principles sometimes conflict – for example, in situations like those facing Mrs. Bergmeier or a person deciding whether to lie to save innocent individuals. In the face of such conflicts, we are sometimes told that conflicts between principles have been anticipated and higher-order principles are in place to resolve such conflicts. For example, it is sometimes argued that we find implicitly or explicitly in religious texts or in the interpretation of those texts by respected religious figures that the saving of an innocent human life takes precedence over not lying if two principles come into conflict. Others, as noted earlier, will turn to God for direct guidance. Still others will consider rationally the consequences of prioritizing the conflicting principles and maximize benefits or minimize harm.

However conflicts are prioritized, the general point for our purposes holds. When we are assessing the rule-based components in lines of reasoning, conflicts among ethical principles must be identified (if not explicitly noted), and we must determine the extent to which we believe that any implicitly or explicitly suggested prioritizations rightly hold in the case in question.

7.2.3 Key Factors Related to Intuition-Based Components

We'll now turn, finally, to the key factors that make the application and assessment of intuition-based components in lines of reasoning related to genetic engineering so complex. As already noted, classical intuitionism is a specific form of rule-based ethical decision-making where the source of the ethical principles on which decisions are made is what is self-evident rather than based on human reason or divine authority. Accordingly, a number of the factors to consider when assessing classical intuitionism are essentially the same as noted above for rule-based components in general: the authority of the source of the relevant ethical principles, the meaning of these principles, the manner in which these principles are applied to the specific issue under consideration, and how these principles are prioritized when offering conflicting responses.

I believe, though, that the nature and scope of the source of the ethical principles that are to guide our behavior in classical intuitionism deserve special attention as they differ from what we find in the other two variants of rule-based decision-making. The basic assumption for ethical principles grounded in human reason is that they are based on rational argumentation that should be convincing to all and, therefore, that these principles apply to all situations/issues, regardless of what seems right or wrong to any individual or is currently acknowledged by a given social, political, or religious group. Likewise, the basic assumption for ethical principles grounded in God's ethical nature is that because God's nature is the authoritative basis for all proper ethical reasoning, these principles apply to all situations/issues, regardless of what seems right or wrong to any individual or currently acknowledged by a given social, political, or religious group.

The situation is more complex when considering the nature and scope of the source of ethical principles in nonreligious classical intuitionism. Many maintain that these self-evident principles are essentially social constructs, infused in us by unconscious cultural conditioning or taught to us early in life by significant others – by parents, religious leaders, school teachers, and/or friends. Others maintain that certain ethical principles (moral sensibilities) – for instance, our belief in fairness or the virtue of empathetic behavior – are innate (inborn).

However, it clearly doesn't follow in either case that self-evident ethical principles can reasonably be considered to be the authoritative basis for all proper ethical reasoning, regardless of what seems right or wrong to any individual or is currently acknowledged by a given social, political, or religious group. In fact, just the opposite appears true. When we couple the claim that self-evident ethical principles are social constructs or innate with the fact that such principles can differ widely from culture to culture and within a culture, we have little reason for assuming that the self-evident ethical principles of a given individual or groups of individuals have any ethical authority for anyone other than the person or group to whom they are self-evident. Or, to focus the relevance of this point on our assessment of intuition-based components in lines of reasoning related to genetic engineering, given a social construct or innate understanding of self-evident ethical principles, there is no justifiable basis for assuming that a perspective being advanced on the basis of these self-evident principles – for example, that it is self-evident that the modification of human traits that will hold for future generations is obviously going too far – should be convincing to those who don't already (or don't on reflection) also find these principles self-evident.

Of course, this doesn't apply to the religious variant of classical intuitionism – which maintains that certain self-evident ethical beliefs (natural laws) have been infused in us as creations of God. In this case, the ethical principles, do, if we grant the authority of the source as true, apply to all, so we again find ourselves facing the question of whether individuals can justifiably consider the divine an authoritative source of ethical truth.

The version of intuitionism based on a direct feeling or sense of what is right might seem the least relevant approach to ethical decision-making for us to consider since few of the lines of reasoning related to genetic engineering in question are explicitly grounded in a direct feeling or sense of what is right (even a direct feeling or sense of what God is telling us directly is right). I don't think this assessment of the relevance of direct intuitionism for our purposes is accurate. As we have seen, there is (1) in rule-based ethical decision-making often the need to prioritize conflicting principles or apply general principles to

specific situations not directly addressed in these principles and (2) in consequence-based decision-making often the need to weight and prioritize projected
consequences. In many such cases, as I've noted, the final response to these
complexities comes down a personal (for some, a personal religious) subjective
feeling.

This direct intuition approach to ethical decision-making is clearly the most
subjective of those we've considered. As noted previously, most consequence-
based and rule-based approaches to ethical decision-making give us responses
that, per hypothesis, *hold* for all of us. Classical intuitionism isn't, per hypothesis,
based on rules that all must accept, but at least the application of the self-evident
principles is at times open to objective consideration. The direct intuition
approach, however, has no aspect that is open to objective consideration, and
this means lines of reasoning incorporating direct intuition components – for
example, a line of reasoning that ultimately ends with the prioritizing of consequences or rules on the basis of each individual's sense of what is the best outcome
overall – offer little basis for maintaining that others ought to agree, and act,
accordingly.

There is, though, a related challenge to the religious version of the direct intuition
approach that merits further discussion. The religious version is less subjective
since that which is felt to be the right response has, per hypothesis, its grounding in
the knowledge and moral nature of God, which can be objectively evaluated as
a valid source of ethical truth. However, those claiming to receive direct divine
guidance in any area – including genetic engineering – at times receive differing,
sometimes contradictory responses. So barring convincing reasons to believe just
certain individuals have received privileged truth, we are left with little reason to
consider these direct revelations to others authoritative for us.

7.3 How Should We Decide These Issues for Ourselves?

Where does all this leave us? The question before us, remember, is how we can
best assess the strength or weakness of the various lines of reasoning related to
human genetic engineering. I've argued to this point that the best way forward
for us as individuals is to identify the consequence-based, rule-based, and
intuition-based components in these lines of reasoning and then assess the
strength and weakness of these components by considering the key complicat-
ing factors related to each component.

What we've found, I believe, is that while it will be very difficult to demonstrate that any of the lines of reasoning we've considered *cannot be justifiably*
maintained or that any of the lines of reasoning *must be* affirmed, the consideration of the key factors related to each component places us in good position to

determine the perceived strength and weakness of each relevant line of reasoning overall and, therefore, in the best epistemic position possible to make justifiable decisions for ourselves.

Of course, few of us will ever be in a position to state definitively that we have considered all relevant lines of reasoning to date in relation to any of the specific issues related to genetic engineering. Furthermore, none of us knows what new data or lines of reasoning will be forthcoming. We need to acknowledge, accordingly, that our perspectives might change, given the consideration of new information or changes in our consequence-based, rule-based and/or intuition-based lens.

I do not find this troubling. The two standard assumptions in most definitions of intellectual humility are that equally sincere, knowledgeable individuals can differ on issues and that any of us can be wrong. Given this reading, the situation we should acknowledge we find ourselves in when assessing the strength and weakness of the lines of reasoning related to genetic engineering is one of intellectual humility. Equally knowledgeable and sincere individuals can justifiably differ on the perceived strength or weakness of the various components in a given line of reasoning, can differ on the perceived overall strength or weaknesses in this line of reasoning, and can differ on the final response to the issues in question, given all relevant lines of reasoning under consideration. Moreover, each of us can be wrong.

I don't think this need give us pause. Being intellectually humble doesn't (in fact, can't) restrict us from making decisions and taking action. William James defined "genuine" choices as those that are "live" (that which is being considered is an actual possibility), "forced" (making a choice that cannot be avoided), and "momentous" (the choice will make a real difference in the world) (Chignell, 2018).

I believe that the decisions we make around genetic engineering are genuine in this sense. We are making decisions about activity that really can occur. We either choose to think about these issues or "have chosen" not to do so, choose to hold a position on these issues or "have chosen" not to do so, and then choose to act upon these decisions or "have chosen" not to do so. And our choices will have a real impact in our world.

Furthermore, approaching these choices with the assumption that equally sincere, knowledgeable individuals can differ and we can be wrong will minimize conscious or unconscious proof-texting. If we believe others can justifiably differ from us and we can be wrong, we are more likely to consider all relevant lines of reasoning comprehensively and openly before making our decisions than to settle on a stance before considering the relevant data and lines of reasoning and then simply selectively using such data and lines of reasoning to support this *a priori* position.

7.4 How Can We Most Productively Engage in Dialog with Others on These Issues?

Approaching genetic engineering in an intellectually humble manner will also affect the way we dialog with others around various issues. When we enter a discussion assuming that we already know the one right answer, it follows that those holding differing perspectives either don't have all the relevant information (aren't aware of the data and lines of reasoning that led us to the "truth") or are consciously or unconsciously unwilling to acknowledge what they actually know to be the case.

Of course, if there is objective evidence for a claim (evidence based on non-question-begging criteria on which almost everyone agrees), then we really do have a strong basis for assuming a person who disagrees doesn't have access to all the relevant data or has some conscious or unconscious reason for holding a position that is actually not defensible. To cite trivial examples, if all the relevant sources of information tell us that a famous person was born in a given year or that a football team won its latest game by a specific margin, then unless a person who claims otherwise has objectively verifiable access to different sources of information, we can assume that the person just hasn't accessed the relevant sources or has some reason for continuing to deny what the evidence clearly demonstrates to be the case – for example, that the person just wants to upset us or make us angry. Accordingly, in cases like this, once we have verified that the same data and lines of reasoning are being considered, we can justifiably explore and challenge our opponents' motives or intentions.

However, if we assume, as I believe has been shown, that attempts to offer lines of reasoning for or against the various aspects of genetic engineering that all rational individuals must accept are not successful – that is, if we assume that sincere, knowledgeable individuals can differ with us on these issues – then we are more likely to focus our discussion on the differing interpretations of the data or differing assumptions we bring to the discussion than to focus on the motives or "agenda" of the person with whom we disagree.

Consider again one last time, for example, the argument that preimplantation embryo selection is wrong because a step in the process requires in vitro fertilization (IVF) and this process normally eventuates in the destruction of embryos, which is ethically wrong because the full right to human life begins at conception. If we assume that there is no line of reasoning based on criteria that most accept that establishes objectively that the right to life does or does not begin at conception, this doesn't mean that we shouldn't share with our opponents the reasons we believe our position is the correct one or even that we shouldn't attempt to have our position codified in law. It does mean, though,

I believe, that we should avoid claiming that those on either side just obviously haven't considered all the relevant information, thought about it in the right way, and/or have questionable motives or intentions tied to some nefarious agenda. This in turn can open the door to respectful dialog, which can, it's been shown, lead to the modification of even firmly held positions.

7.5 Where Is God in All This?

In closing, let's revisit the question of where God is in all this. I've argued that attempting to identify *the* current stance of a religion on issues related to genetic engineering is problematic because the differing beliefs on genetic engineering among the variants within a religion are often as great as or even greater than the differing beliefs among religions. I've also argued that simply polling self-identified adherents of a religion on their views on genetic engineering can be interesting but problematic because this doesn't give us a basis for determining if the person holds this view for a religious reason and, if so, what that reason is. What I've done, instead, is to explore the religious beliefs (beliefs that have a religious basis) and related lines of reasoning on genetic engineering apart from the religion or variant in which these beliefs are found or the extent to which individuals who self-report as adherents to a religion or a variant actually hold these religious beliefs and related lines of reasoning.

What have we found in this regard? We have seen that in some ways the lines of reasoning containing a religious aspect don't differ significantly from lines of reasoning not containing a religious aspect. The key consequence-based considerations in both cases generally focus on the actual and potential benefits for, and risks to, human health and well-being; the key rule-based considerations in both normally focus on the ethical principles of nonmaleficence (do no harm) and beneficence (do good); and the key intuition-based considerations in both center focus on the concept of self-evidency. So complexities inherent in these three approaches to ethical decision-making apply to both religious and non-religious variants of these approaches in lines of reasoning related to genetic engineering.

What does differ significantly is the basis (source, grounding) for the ethical guidance offered in each of these three approaches to ethical decision-making. The consequence-based, rule-based, and/or intuition-based lines of reasoning with religious aspects ground their ethical authority in divine truth – in how God or the Divine, through religious texts, religious tradition, and/or direct privileged communication would have us make ethical decisions. The lines of reasoning without religious aspects have their ethical grounding in human reason and/or self-evidency.

I've argued, though, that grounding ethical decisions in divine truth is no less (or more) justified than grounding ethical decisions in human reason or self-evidency. When coupling this with the significance of human genetic engineering for our future, and the fact that dialog around these issues can impact belief and action, we have a very sound basis for continuing to consider religious perspectives as seriously as nonreligious perspectives as we individually and together grapple with the ethics of human genetic engineering.

References

AgBiotechNet. (2001). Religious Beliefs Influence Views of Genetic Engineering, www.cabi.org/agbiotechnet/news/523.

American Human. (2021). Animals in Research, www.americanhumane.org/position-statement/animals-in-research/.

Arcata, J. (2021). If Mosquitoes Were Eradicated, What Would Be the Consequences? *NewScientist*, www.newscientist.com/lastword/mg25233643-900-if-mosquitoes-were-eradicated-what-would-be-the-consequences/.

Basinger, D. (2020a). Religious Diversity (Pluralism). *The Stanford Encyclopedia of Philosophy*, https://plato.stanford.edu/archives/win2020/entries/religious-pluralism/.

Basinger, D. (2020b). Affirmative Position: It is Reasonable to Believe That Only One Religion is True. In Peterson, M. & VanArragon, R., eds., *Contemporary Debates in Philosophy of Religion*. Oxford: Wiley Blackwell, pp. 243–252.

Basinger, D. (2013). Introduction to Open Theism. In Diller, J. & Kasher, A., eds. *Models of God and Alternative Ultimate Realities*. New York: Springer, pp. 263–274.

Beard, M. (2020). Ethics Explorer: Judgment and Moral Intuition. *The Ethics Center*, https://ethics.org.au/ethics-explainer-ethical-judgement-and-moral-intuition/ Biotechnical.

Bergman, M. (2019). Perspectives on Gene Editing. *Harvard Gazette*, https://news.harvard.edu/gazette/story/2019/01/perspectives-on-gene-editing/ (Bergman, 2019).

Britannica. (2020). Categorical Imperative. *Encyclopedia Britannica*, www.britannica.com/topic/categorical-imperative.

Brokowski C. & Adli M. (2019) CRISPR Ethics: Moral Considerations for Applications of a Powerful Tool. *Science Direct*, www.sciencedirect.com/science/article/abs/pii/S0022283618305862.

Callaway, E. (2018). Controversial CRISPR "Gene Drives" Tested in Mammals for the First Time. *Nature*, www.nature.com/articles/d41586-018-05665-1.

Chignell, A. (2018). The Ethics of Belief. *The Stanford Encyclopedia of Philosophy*, https://plato.stanford.edu/entries/ethics-belief/.

Civilsdaily. (2019). What Are the Ethical Concerns Involved in Gene Editing Technology? www.civilsdaily.com/mains/what-are-the-ethical-concerns-involved-in-gene-editing-technology-discuss/.

Coffey, D. (2020). What is a Gene Drive? *LIVESCI=NCE*, www.livescience.com/gene-drive.html.

Cohen, J. (2019). China's CRISPR Push in Animals Promises Better Meat, Novel Therapies, and Pig Organs for People. *Science*, www.science.org/content/article/china-s-crispr-push-animals-promises-better-meat-novel-therapies-and-pig-organs-people.

Conserve Future Energy. (n.d.). Pros and Cons of Genetically Modified Organisms (GMO's), www.conserve-energy-future.com/pros-cons-gmos.php.

Corbyn, Z. (2021). Is It Possible to Change a Chicken's Sex before It Hatches? *The Guardian*, www.theguardian.com/food/2021/jan/31/good-vibrations-sound-waves-eggs-ethical-slaughter-male-chicks.

Dalechek, D. (2021). CRISPR and the Brain, *Integrated DNA Technologies*, www.idtdna.com/pages/community/blog/post/crispr-and-the-brain.

DerSarkissian, C. (2022). Should You Screen Your Genes before You Conceive? *Grow by WebMD*, www.webmd.com/baby/genetic-tests-before-pregnancy.

Doudna, J. & Sternberg, S. (2017). *A Crack in Creation: Gene Editing and the Unthinkable Power to Control Evolution*, Boston: Mariner Books.

Dunning, H. (2021). Simple Genetic Modification Aims to Stop Mosquitoes Spreading Malaria. *Imperial College London*, www.imperial.ac.uk/news/219394/simple-genetic-modification-aims-stop-mosquitoes/.

Eikelboom, R. (2011). Why Did God Create Mosquitoes? *Think Christian*, https://thinkchristian.net/why-did-god-create-mosquitoes/discussion.

Evans, J. (2021). Setting Ethical Limits on Human Gene Editing after the Fall of the Somatic/Germline Barrier. *PNAS*, 118(22). https://doi.org/10.1073/pnas.2004837117.

Fertility Center. (n.d.). Preimplantation Genetic Testing (PGT). *Fertility and Reproductive Center*, https://fertility.wustl.edu/treatments-services/genetic-counseling/preimplantation-genetic-testing-pgt/.

Fletcher, J. (1966). *Situation Ethic: The New Morality*. Louisville: Westminster John Knox Press.

Fliesler, N. (2020). After Decades of Evolution, Gene Therapy Arrives. *Boston Children's Hospital*, https://answers.childrenshospital.org/gene-therapy-history.

Gardner, A. (2020). Your Guide to Prenatal Testing. *Grow by WedMD*, www.webmd.com/baby/your-guide-prenatal-testing.

Genes and Health. (n.d.). Genes Made Easy. *Genes & Health*, www.genesandhealth.org/genes-your-health/genes-made-easy.

Genetics and Society. (2006). Inheritable Genetic Modification Arguments Pro and Con. *Center for Genetics and Society*, www.geneticsandsociety.org/internal-content/inheritable-genetic-modification-arguments-pro-and-con.

Genome Research. (2017). What Are the Ethical Concerns of Genome Editing? *NIH National Genome Research Institute*, www.genome.gov/about-genom ics/policy-issues/Genome-Editing/ethical-concerns.

Goodyear Chiropractic. (2019). Stem Cell Therapy: Is it Safe? www.goodyear health.com/resources/blog/stem-cell-therapy-is-it-safe/.

Gragnolati, A. (2022). What Are the Pros and Cons of Gene Therapy? *GoodRx Health*, www.goodrx.com/health-topic/gene-therapy/gene-therapy-pros-cons.

Gynyell, C. & Douglas, T. (2014). Stocking the Genetic Supermarket: Reproductive Genetic Technologies and Collective Action Problems. *National Library of Medicine*, www.ncbi.nlm.nih.gov/pmc/articles/PMC4402029/.

Hryhorowicz, M., Zeyland, J., Slomski, R. & Lipinski, D. (2017). Genetically Modified Pigs as Organ Donors for Xenotransplantation. *National Library of Medicine*, www.ncbi.nlm.nih.gov/pmc/articles/PMC5617878/.

Human Subjects Protection. (n.d.). Resolving Conflicts between Ethical Principles. *Yale University Human Subjects Protection*, https://assessment-module.yale.edu/human-subjects-protection/resolving-conflicts-between-ethical-principles.

Hunter, J. (2022). Three Ethical Issues around Pig Heart Transplants. *BBC News*, www.bbc.com/news/world-59951264.

Innovation. (n.d.). Genetically Engineered Animals: Frequently Asked Questions. *Biotechnology Innovation Organization*, https://archive.bio.org/ articles/genetically-engineered-animals-frequently-asked-questions.

Johnson, T. (2019). Human Genetic Enhancement Might Soon be Possible – but Where Do You Draw the Line? *The Conversation*, https://theconversation .com/human-genetic-enhancement-might-soon-be-possible-but-where-do-we-draw-the-line-127406.

Karj, T. (2013). The Role of Virtue Ethics in Determining Acceptable Limits of Genetic Enhancement. *Theological Research*, https://czasopisma.upjp2.edu .pl/theologicalresearch/article/view/154.

Kelmer, S. & Lohr, A. (2022). Cell & Gene Therapy Investment Outlook in 2022 & beyond. *Cell & Gene*, www.cellandgene.com/doc/cell-gene-therap ies-investment-outlook-in-beyond-0001.

Kozlov, M. (2022). Clinical Trials for Pig-to-Human Organ Transplants Inch Closer. *Nature*, www.nature.com/articles/d41586-022-01861-2.

Lagay, F. (2000). Is Genetic Enhancement a Gift to Future Generations? *AMA Journal of Ethics*, https://journalofethics.ama-assn.org/article/genetic-enhancement-gift-future-generations/2000-12.

Locke, L. (2020). The Promise of CRISPR for Human Germline Editing and the Perils of "Playing God." *National Library of Medicine*, www.ncbi.nlm.nih .gov/pmc/articles/PMC7047104/.

Living Oceans. (n.d.). Genetically Modified Salmon, https://livingoceans.org/initiatives/salmon-farming/issues/genetically-modified-salmon.

Lui, S. (2020). Legal Reflections on the Case of Genome-Edited Babies. *Global Health Research and Policy*, https://ghrp.biomedcentral.com/articles/10.1186/s41256-020-00153-4.

Mayo Clinic. (n.d.). Gene Therapy. www.mayoclinic.org/tests-procedures/gene-therapy/about/pac-20384619.

MedlinePlus. (n.d.). How Does Gene Therapy Work? *National Library of Medicine*, https://medlineplus.gov/genetics/understanding/therapy/proced ures/.

Melillo, G. (2022). A Look at the Current, Future State of Cell and Gene Therapies in the United States. *AJMC*, www.ajmc.com/view/a-look-at-the-current-future-state-of-cell-and-gene-therapies-in-the-united-states.

Missouri School of Medicine. (n.d.). Gene Therapy and Genetic Engineering. *Center for Health Ethics*, https://medicine.missouri.edu/centers-institutes-labs/health-ethics/faq/gene-therapy.

McQueen, H. (2022). The 10 Most Expensive Drugs in the US, Period. *GoodRx Health*, www.goodrx.com/healthcare-access/drug-cost-and-savings/most-expensive-drugs-period.

National Human Genome Research Institute. (n.d.). Cloning Fact Sheet, www.genome.gov/about-genomics/policy-issues/Genome-Editing/ethical-concerns.

NewScientist. (2022). CRISPR: A Technology That Can Be Used to Edit Genes, .www.newscientist.com/definition/what-is-crispr/.

Patterson, R., Rothstein, J. & Barbey, A. (2012). Reasoning, Cognitive Control, and Moral Intuition. *Frontiers in Integrative Neuroscience*, www.frontiersin.org/articles/10.3389/fnint.2012.00114/full.

Pew Trust. (2001). Views on Genetic Modification of Food Influenced by Religious Beliefs, Not Just Science, www.pewtrusts.org/en/about/news-room/press-releases-and-statements/2001/07/26/views-on-genetic-modifica tion-of-food-influenced-by-religious-beliefs-not-just-science.

Pew Research Center. (2016a). U.S. Public Opinion on the Future of Gene Editing, www.pewresearch.org/science/2016/07/26/u-s-public-opinion-on-the-future-use-of-gene-editing/.

Pew Research Center. (2016b). Human Enhancement: The Scientific and Ethical Dimensions of Striving for Perfection, www.pewresearch.org/sci ence/2016/07/26/human-enhancement-the-scientific-and-ethical-dimen sions-of-striving-for-perfection/.

Qaiser, F. (2020). Study: There Is No Country Where Heritable Human Genome Editing Is Permitted. *Forbes*, www.forbes.com/sites/farahqaiser/2020/10/31/

study-there-is-no-country-where-heritable-human-genome-editing-is-permit ted/?sh=64d143327617.

Questions. (n.d.). How Should a Christian View Genetic Engineering? *Got Questions*, www.gotquestions.org/genetic-engineering.html.

Ramamoorth, M. & Narvekar, A. (2015). Non Viral Vectors in Gene Therapy: An Overview. *NIH National Library of Medicine*, www.ncbi.nlm.nih.gov/ pmc/articles/PMC4347098.

Reardon, S. (2020). Step Aside CRISPR, RNA Editing is Taking Off. *Nature*, www.nature.com/articles/d41586-020-00272-5.

Regalodo, A. (2019). China's CRISPR Twins Might Have Had Their Brains Inadvertently Enhanced. *MIT Technology Review*, www.technologyreview .com/2019/02/21/137309/the-crispr-twins-had-their-brains-altered/.

Rosner, F. (1999). Pig Organs for Transplantation into Humans: A Jewish View. *Mount Sinai Journal of Medicine*, https://read.qxmd.com/read/10618731/ pig-organs-for-transplantation-into-humans-a-jewish-view (Rosner, 1999).

Savulescu, J. (2015). Five Reasons We Should Embrace Gene-Editing Research on Human Embryos. *PHY-ORG*, https://phys.org/news/2015-12-embrace-gene-editing-human-embryos.html.

Shellnutt, K. (2020). Engineered in His Image? Christians More Cautious about Gene Editing. *Christianity Today*, www.christianitytoday.com/news/2020/ december/pew-survey-global-bioethics-gene-editing-crispr-christians.html (Shellnutt, 2020).

Sigma Repository. (2021). NPWH Position Statement: Prepregnancy Genetic Carrier Screening, https://sigma.nursingrepository.org/handle/10755/ 21543.

Spina bifida. (n.d.). Spina Bifida: Disease at a Glance. *National Center for Advancing Translational Sciences*, https://rarediseases.info.nih.gov/dis eases/7673/spina-bifida.

StopGM. (2019). The Pros and Cons of Genetically Modified Animals, https:// stopgm.org.uk/the-pros-and-cons-of-genetically-modified-animals/.

Stratton-Lake, P. (2020). Intuitionism in Ethics. *The Stanford Encyclopedia of Philosophy, Zalta*, https://plato.stanford.edu/archives/sum2020/entries/intu itionism-ethics/ (Stratton-Lake, 2020).

Study.com. (2022). Animal Cloning, https://study.com/learn/lesson/animal-cloning-process-pros-cons.html (Study, 2022).

Synthego. (n.d.). CRISPR in Agriculture: An Era of Food Evolution, www .synthego.com/blog/crispr-agriculture-foods.

Torrella, K. (2022). Gene Editing Could Upend the Future of Factory Farming – for Better or Worse. *Vox*, www.vox.com/22994946/gene-editing-farm-ani mals-livestock-crispr-genetic-engineering.

UFDA. (2022). How Gene Therapy Can Cure or Treat Diseases. *US Food and Drug Administration*, www.fda.gov/consumers/consumer-updates/how-gene-therapy-can-cure-or-treat-diseases.

USDA. (2022). Recent Trends in GE Adoption. *US Department of Agriculture*, www.ers.usda.gov/data-products/adoption-of-genetically-engineered-crops-in-the-u-s/recent-trends-in-ge-adoption/.

UK Health System. (n.d.). Preconception and Prenatal Genetic Counseling. *University of Kansas Health System*, www.kansashealthsystem.com/care/specialties/maternal-fetal-medicine/preconception-prenatal-genetic-counseling.

Yg Topics. (2021). What is Gene Therapy? www.yourgenome.org/facts/what-is-gene-therapy/.

Wallace, J. (2021). If Mosquitoes Were Eradicated, What Would Be the Consequences? *NewScientist*, www.newscientist.com/lastword/mg25233643-900-if-mosquitoes-were-eradicated-what-would-be-the-consequences/.

Warmflash, D. (2019). Religious Beliefs Shape Our Thinking on Cloning, Stem Cells, and Gene Editing. *Church and State*, https://churchandstate.org.uk/2019/11/religious-beliefs-shape-our-thinking-on-cloning-stem-cells-and-gene-editing/.

Wright, G. & Lavery, T. (n.d.). Scientific Method. *TechTarget*, www.techtarget.com/whatis/definition/scientific-method.

Cambridge Elements ≡

The Problems of God

Series Editor
Michael L. Peterson
Asbury Theological Seminary

Michael Peterson is Professor of Philosophy at Asbury Theological Seminary. He is the author of *God and Evil* (Routledge); *Monotheism, Suffering, and Evil* (Cambridge University Press); *With All Your Mind* (University of Notre Dame Press); *C. S. Lewis and the Christian Worldview* (Oxford University Press); *Evil and the Christian God* (Baker Book House); and *Philosophy of Education: Issues and Options* (Intervarsity Press). He is co-author of *Reason and Religious Belief* (Oxford University Press); *Science, Evolution, and Religion: A Debate about Atheism and Theism* (Oxford University Press); and *Biology, Religion, and Philosophy* (Cambridge University Press). He is editor of *The Problem of Evil: Selected Readings* (University of Notre Dame Press). He is co-editor of *Philosophy of Religion: Selected Readings* (Oxford University Press) and *Contemporary Debates in Philosophy of Religion* (Wiley-Blackwell). He served as General Editor of the Blackwell monograph series *Exploring Philosophy of Religion* and is founding Managing Editor of the journal *Faith and Philosophy*.

About the Series

This series explores problems related to God, such as the human quest for God or gods, contemplation of God, and critique and rejection of God. Concise, authoritative volumes in this series will reflect the methods of a variety of disciplines, including philosophy of religion, theology, religious studies, and sociology.

Cambridge Elements ≡

The Problems of God

Elements in the Series

A full series listing is available at: www.cambridge.org/EPOG

Printed in the United States
by Baker & Taylor Publisher Services